Simply the Best

Guaranteeing the Best Possible Outcome

Exceptional Project Performance

How to ensure that your project achieves what you
want it to achieve

Philip E. Le G. Baylis

authorHOUSE®

T0370537

AuthorHouse™ UK Ltd.
1663 Liberty Drive
Bloomington, IN 47403 USA
www.authorhouse.co.uk
Phone: 0800.197.4150

Published by AuthorHouse   03/14/2014

ISBN: 978-1-4490-6240-8 (sc)
ISBN: 978-1-4670-0665-1 (e)

Forth print run Jan 2014
Third print run June 2009 Limited Edition
Second print run August 2007
First print run Feb 2007 Limited Edition

This book is dedicated to

Caroline, Mark and Nicola

Contents

Foreword

How will this book benefit you?

Do you want to achieve the *best possible outcome* for both your business and also your projects?

Do you want *exceptional performance*?

If so then you should read and implement the techniques in this book.

This book explains how the best possible outcome, and exceptional performance can be obtained for your:
- Business
- Projects
- Functions/Departments
- Operations
- Initiatives
- Teams

All of these are projects, and can be managed as projects. This book is about how to project manage your business to get the best possible outcome and thereby achieve exceptional performance. These are the results that will make your clients' believe that your business is remarkable.

By applying what is in this book you will outstrip your competitors, increase market share, improved turnover, improve profits and satisfy your clients.

This book explains 5 key techniques that will make a significant improvement to your project performance. It will explain how you can get the best possible outcome.

Is there a *single* issue that is holding any project back from achieving its full potential? If there is wouldn't you wish to know what it is?

What is the single issue that is holding your project back from achieving exceptional performance?

To achieve improved project performance then understanding what holds people back from really being successful in their lives and at work, is essential. For a project to really perform, and achieve its full potential, its staff, and the project leader, must perform their best. The staff are the most important asset within any business. It is this human element that is essential for achieving success.

What is holding your people back from performing and succeeding in their lives?

How can we align people to the business and how can we get the best out of them?

This book is a journey. All profit making projects are on a journey of discovery. This book will enable you to take your project on this journey to really achieve exceptional results and outstrip any competitors.

With the commitment, vision and drive of the top directors and project leaders, and by releasing the energies of their staff then outstanding results can be achieved by using these 5 techniques.

My experience

I have been in the project management world for over 37 years as a professional chartered engineer. In all this time I have worked with a consulting company and a major contracting company, both based in the UK from between 1974 and 2011.

I have also been working for a Business School for the last 13 years on an MBA module in Project Management. I have been teaching professional MBA students on how to project manage their business and get their best possible outcome.

I also run my own consultancy business to help organisations to project manage their business.

My project management experience includes being on the design and construction teams of very large and complex £5bn, 30 year projects, to very simple £10,000, 2 week projects.

My expertise covers the project management of businesses, organisations, functions, teams and people. I have been involved with project management of large design and construction projects such as power stations, tunnels, roads, bridges, foundations, maintenance projects, research and development, development and implementation of software. Also business project management, such as setting up organisations, setting up teams, implementing initiatives and organisational change. This experience has been gained in the UK, Africa, Middle East and Far East.

In the last 15 years, I have been developing and using techniques that make a significant improvement in organisational behaviour and performance.

I am a "Jonah" which means I am fully trained in the techniques of Theory of Constraints developed by Eli Goldratt. These techniques developed my logical understanding of organisations, many of the techniques in this book have been developed from this logical thinking.

I realised that in order to get the best possible outcome, there has to be a change in the way we treat and manage people within businesses. I have therefore expanded my understanding of people by becoming a Master Coach, Master NLP practitioner, Neuro-Linguistic Programming, and trained to an intermediate level in psychotherapy.

This book is the result of my experiences with organisational development and people development and subsequent knowledge of how to get the best possible outcome and achieve exceptional performance.

How to use this book

This book has been laid out to enable you to note down your own thoughts within the margins or the blank pages.

The chapters should be read one per day. At the end of the chapter blank pages have been provided with a summary and questions to record your own experiences, thoughts and actions.

Introduction

1   Introduction

1.1   Introduction to 5PM

A number of my professional students said that the project management module, of the Business Engineering MBA course that I run, provides a different dimension to project management.

My students said that this perspective had given them a considerable insight into the practical issues of project management when working with people, that no current project management text covered this material and hence they urged me to publish a book that did.

This book is the result of that feedback.

Five aspects of project management (5PM)—5 of the best

There is a widely quoted figure that states:

"80% of all projects worldwide fail to achieve time, cost and quality."

If this is the case then the project management techniques and skills, that are currently taught and being practised, are necessary but insufficient.

These are basics of project management and include:
1. Integration management
2. Scope management
3. Time management
4. Cost management
5. Quality management
6. HR management
7. Risk management
8. Procurement management
9. Communications management
10. Stakeholder management

---

80 percent of all projects worldwide fail to achieve time, cost and quality

---

What are these 5 techniques? These techniques are identified, in Fig 1.1, and have to be fully satisfied to achieve the best outcome or result for the project.

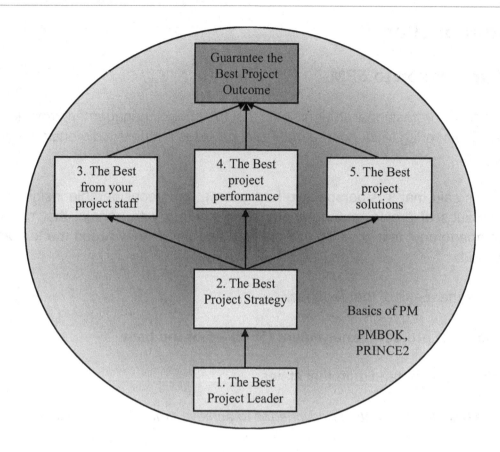

Fig 1.1 The 5 techniques (5PM) that will deliver the best possible outcome

Systems and people

If a project has the best systems but no people, then the project cannot perform at all. However, if the project has the best people, who are committed, motivated, enthusiastic, focused, but no systems, then the people will make things happen and probably achieve 80% of the project's potential.

If the project has the best people, who are committed, enthusiastic, positive, they will ensure the best outcome is achieved

So, if this is the case, then why is the main focus of project management on the systems and the processes?

A lot of our project management techniques focus mainly on the systems, but project management is about people and managing them effectively.

We should be focusing on people first and systems second. We must create the right culture, in which the project leader can lead, motivate his staff, and create an environment where core issues are resolved, and achieve the best project performance.

Guaranteeing the best possible outcome

The title of this book is *Guaranteeing the Best Possible Outcome*. It is impossible to guarantee anything that has not yet happened, especially in project management. So this book is not claiming that the outcome of a project can be guaranteed, but only the **best** outcome for the project given the circumstances in which the project is being carried out.

In project management we have to work within the external constraints that exist.

These include:
- o   Natural constraints - earthquakes, tsunamis, extreme weather
- o   Market constraints - availability of good staff, pricing levels, supply
- o   Client constraints - ways of doing things, contract conditions
- o   Business constraints - policies, availability and standard of staff and resources, cost estimates, ways of doing things, systems.

Given these constraints, we should be able to guarantee the best outcome for our project, achieving the project's potential within the limitation of these constraints. If we had other resources, then we may achieve a different or improved outcome.

This book is about making the very most from what we have in order to achieve the best outcome.

1.2   Readers

Who will benefit from reading this book?
Who this book is aimed at? Who isn't it aimed at?

This book explains specific aspects, skills or abilities, in addition to the basic project management skills, that are needed to ensure a project achieves the best possible outcome.

The basics of project management are not covered here since those skills and techniques are well documented in other texts.

The people who would benefit from this book are those who manage teams of any size and are keen to understand additional aspects such as:

- o   having the best project leader
- o   having the best strategic thinking

- o getting the best out of people
- o achieving the best potential performance
- o developing the best solution

This book gives a different dimension to project management and helps leaders and mangers to have a better understanding of people and how to get the best out of them to deliver the best result.

1.3   Purpose of this book

Why has this book been written?

This book aims to provide the project management community with material covering additional key aspects and techniques.

This book will help project managers to finish their projects on time and in full, they will have achieved the best possible outcome and that their projects will have achieved their full potential to the client's satisfaction.

1.4   Outcome of this book

What is the learning outcome of this book?

The learning outcome of this book is for the project managers who read, and understand the skills and techniques, to be able to apply them, maybe with some help, to their project and achieve success. There will be times when extra help will be needed to ensure the techniques are applied effectively. I will provide this support.

The focus of this book is to help project leaders to deliver results and be successful.

But to get started we have to understand what a project is and the context within which it is being carried out, this is covered in chapter 2.

Project Context

2   Project Context

The context of a project may have a significant effect on the outcome of the project and inhibit the project leader from achieving its true potential.

But before we consider the context, we have to define the word "project".

2.1   Project Definition

What do we mean by a project?

A project is defined as:

- o having a defined lifecycle with predetermined stages
  - inception (feasibility, defining)
  - doing (design, development, construction, building)
  - close (testing, commissioning, handover)
- o having a single point of responsibility for deliver, e.g. a project leader
- o being unique in nature, hasn't been done before, or not recently
- o having a clear defined outcome and reason for existence

A project is unique, with defined outcome and reason, with a leader who is responsible for the project achievement.

However, the conditions that have to be satisfied while executing the project are:

- o must be done safely and environmentally
- o the staff have the appropriate skills, and are able to do their task
- o they have the appropriate kit and equipment to carry out their tasks effectively, and are capable of doing their tasks.
- o They must ensure that they can deliver to a defined quality and standard.

The project is done safely, and environmentally, with appropriate skills, the right equipment and to the appropriate standard

---

In fact a project can be anything that is unique. It can be either a product or service or result. It is temporary, and has a defined outcome.

Projects can be for profit or non-profit, the non-profit projects can be difficult to manage and will not be considered further.

Historically projects that are for profit were defined in terms of the 3 elements of time, budget, quality or standards. I have included a 4th element which is client's satisfaction, or creating value, understanding and satisfying their needs. Success is the delivery of each of these elements.

Fig 2.1 The 4 elements of PM. Time, budget, standards, client's satisfaction and needs, success

---

A project is carried out to time, budget, and standard, with customer needs satisfied, and success achieved

---

Of these 4 elements which is the most important?

Can a project be on time and within budget but dissatisfy the client? Yes.
Can a project overrun time and budget, and still satisfy the client? Yes.

The most important is satisfying the client, within the context of any contractual agreement, whilst still doing one's best with time, budget and quality/standards.

2.2 Project types

A project creates a change in a business that then delivers a different business result.

All strategies within a business are there to create a change in business performance. Therefore, all strategic outcomes are a project within themselves. Also, as businesses are there to deliver different outcomes or results each year then the business is also a project.

This definition of a project could apply to almost anything in our lives such as:

Traditional types of project are:-
- o Building of any type: housing, office blocks
- o Design and construction of any type: tunnels, roads, airports, stadiums, rail construction, ports
- o Building and maintaining yachts, boats, planes, rockets, satellites
- o Developing and installing software, ERP, SAP
- o Research and development, new products
- o Contract performance, achieving the required profit

However, as all businesses can be managed as a project then business projects could be:-
- o Developing and establishing a new business
- o Company development, achieving a vision and mission, strategic outcomes
- o Company performance, achieving additional turnover and profit results, increasing market share, annual outcomes
- o Acquisition, take over of another business, merger
- o New clients, new markets, new countries, increase turnover and market share
- o Increasing profit, reducing costs
- o New product development, R&D—Market analysis, design development, product development, product testing and commissioning, marketing to achieve initial sales targets, production to meet initial targets (each of these phases can be a project with different project managers)
- o New initiatives, new productivity performance, change management, transformation, change in culture
- o Re-organisation, downsizing, outsourcing
- o Installation and use of new equipment, plant
- o New software design and implementation
- o Specific orders for products, manufacture and shipping, for new/regular clients, one-off or repeat or regular orders
- o New plant installation, new facilities
- o Improved functional or departmental performance achieving an outcome
- o Setting-up new teams, setting up new call centre, setting up new offices, team performance achieving an outcome
- o Shut-down for maintenance
- o Annual maintenance schedule
- o Recruitment of staff for specific projects
- o Design development
- o Manufacturing of any goods
- o Event management
- o Delivering a service
- o Bidding and winning new work
- o Procurement for specific projects, purchase orders
- o Course development, training courses

Other types of project could be:
- Running a country, elections
- Running Europe
- Achieving an MBA
- Career development
- MasterChef event
- Producing Films
- Drug development
- Throwing a party
- Organising a holiday
- Trip overseas
- Rearing of children
- Organising a wedding
- Competitive sailing, sailing to achieve a destination
- Hiking, climbing event
- Mowing the lawn
- Shopping

Many of these projects, identified above, have developed their own systems, processes that are appropriate for their industry, however they still will apply the 10 basic headings of PM outlined by PMBOK/PRINCE2.

Also they may have different drivers of time, budget, standards, client satisfaction depending upon the industry and circumstances of the project.

Many of the techniques discussed, in the following chapters, are directly transferable to operational functions within a business giving that function significant benefits in performance.

Even portfolio and programme management of projects, could be managed as a project using many of these techniques.

Everything in a developing business is a project

A project could be almost anything that we do in our day-to-day lives. So all of us are, to a certain extent, project leaders because we are focusing on getting things done, we are focusing on achieving a certain outcome.

Some projects must be completed to time and cost in order to make a profit. Other projects deliver an outcome, but have no timescale or budget—these are the non-profit projects, which are difficult to complete.

The projects that we will be considering in this book are those that have to be done to a timescale and to a cost or budget. These are profit-making projects.

The attributes of project leader very much depends on:
- the size and complexity of the project
- the culture or country in which the project is being carried out
- the maturity level of the industry
- the maturity of the individual business within that industry

---

The type of project leader chosen needs to reflect the size, complexity, culture, industry and the maturity of the business

---

Different countries and different industries are at different maturity levels of project management. The attributes of the project leader has to reflect the maturity level of the industry and business in which his project is being conducted. If a business and project leader are appointed from overseas, and if their project management culture is different to that of the host country and industry, then they will have difficulty in completing or managing the project.

2.3   Project Size and Complexity

How does project size and complexity affect the approach to project management?

Simple projects

There are many projects that are small, simple and straightforward. The outcome is a simple task and there may be just one or two people, a small team, involved with achieving that task to a certain short timescale.

Simple projects have straightforward tasks, short timescales, and small teams

---

The project manager of that type of project may not necessarily have to deal with team issues. He just ensures that the tasks are carried out in the right way, to the right quality, to the required timescale, so the interpersonal skills that the project manager needs to have may be very limited. He is task focused.

Complex projects

But at the other end of the scale, when you have a complex project with thousands of people involved, lasting for several years, then the project leader has to have different skills.

The more complex the project, the more the project leader needs interpersonal skills to motivate their staff, and the systems/processes will have to be developed.

The leader has to be able to align his staff to the project outcome and purpose, ensure that they understand their role and outcome, motivate them, support them and ensure everyone is working together to actually deliver that complex outcome.

The leader needs to be purpose-focused, values-based and enable their staff to be informed and empowered to take the right decisions quickly.

With complex projects, there may be other external influences which affect that project which he must take into account. These may include pressures from politicians, the Health and Safety Executive, pressure groups or other community groups.

Complex projects need clear outcomes, timescales and team roles

---

These all have to be taken into account by the project leader if the project is going to be successful. So the skill set required, of the project leader, for a complex project, is very different to a skill set for a very simple task orientated short-term project. In this case he spends most of his time on relationship and aligning his teams, the project tasks are done by others.

There is a whole range of different attributes which sets the simple project apart from the complex project. The project leader on complex projects will spend most of his time on relationships whilst the tasks are done by others.

Project type

The type of project has a bearing as well. What is the project there to achieve, what is the scope, it could be highly technical, it could be to do with software, it could be to do with petrochemicals or shipping. Having knowledge of the industry and the tasks involved can be hugely important.

The size, complexity and type of project will very much determine the type of project leader we must have. In order to get the best possible outcome we must have the right role, and the right personality match of the project leader to the role.

If the project leader's personality does not fit the role, the project will not necessarily deliver its full potential, and I will be spending quite a bit of time discussing this issue.

Portfolio of Projects

This is determining what the portfolio, or programme, of projects that are needed to achieve the business's vision. The portfolio has to align to the business's strategy and business plan, and have the skill set, capability and ability to complete the projects.

2.4   Project development

The maturity level of the industry within which the project is being carried out varies considerably across the different industries and also within different countries.

What are the project development stages?
What are the cultural influences?

In the UK the project management approach within the construction industry has developed considerably over the last 10-20 years. The culture has been changing from an aggressive claims culture to one of working together.

Below is a project management development or maturity model which describes four stages of development, Fig 2.2

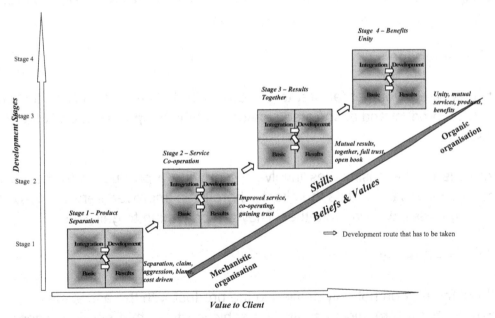

Fig 2.2 Project Management Development Model

Stage One—Product

Stage 1 is at the bottom end of the scale where the industry is very much in a blame culture, this creates divisions between the companies involved, the contractual differences that exist between the company and supply chain, and differences between other contracted parties on that particular project.

A business is engaged to provide a defined product—making, manufacturing, building, researching and developing, constructing. They are given a contract and they tend to hide behind that contract, and deliver the specification.

If there is any difference of opinion, or change to requirements, then the business will claim for additional income. The main driver is to maximise profit, recover their costs. Profit comes first at this level. They will blame each other if there is a lack of clarity or instructions.

At this level you create separation, you create a negative type of culture, there is aggression, there is blame between the business and between the client and the provider.

The project is delivering the specified product and no more, it is cost/profit driven. There is little or no trust. This is the cost world rather than the throughput world.

But who suffers? The client gets a more expensive product, the businesses involved may manage to recover their costs, but there is a lack of trust and poor reputation that may affect the future work load for that business.

Stage Two—Service

Stage two is where you get far greater co-operation between the client, the business producing the product and associated service, and the supply chain and other involved businesses.

The project is for the businesses involved to provide a product, with the associated enhanced service that satisfies the client. There is an improved service, co-operation, closer togetherness, working together. They are beginning to gain trust.

Stage Three—Results

Stage three focuses on not only delivering the product with the associated service, but also ensures that the required results are achieved from that service. These are the results the client actually wants, which may be different to what he may have stated.

So this level ensures the businesses involved work together to create mutual beneficial results for both the client, the businesses providing the service, and the supply chain. There is cost transparency, full trust has to be earned.

Stage Four—Benefits

Stage four is achieving the benefits. To do this there must be unity between the businesses involved. It is working together, as one, to develop mutual services, products that give results and benefits to the client. Whatever the benefits that the clients needs, it is creating the right services and products to deliver those benefits.

The client, the businesses and supply chain are creating these benefits together as if they are all working in the same organisation. There is complete unity and there is no visible difference between the various organisations involved because they are all working as one team to achieve whatever benefits are required.

Mechanistic to organic

As the business develops up this four stage development model, it goes from stage 1 which is a mechanistic business, one which just tells people what to do. They work from procedures, they are told the task to do and if there is a cog that doesn't work within that mechanistic system, then that cog, or person, is replaced and a new one brought in and set to work.

This is where there is very little recognition of what people can do, there is no belief in their people. They are treated as mechanical parts.

The leadership style is often transactional "do as I say", with top-down initiatives.

Stage 2 is where there are processes that define how the business works and partnering is often used. This is where information flow process is important to define.

Stage 3 is where people, including the supply chain, are integrated to deliver a common outcome. The processes become of less importance, outcomes more important.

As the business develops up to stage 4 then the business has become an organic one. This where there is a recognition that the people are the key asset.

People in this type of business fully know, understand, and believe in the mission, vision and values of the business. They are aligned and focused on the delivery of their outcomes and purpose, they are supported and are being developed. They don't need processes or procedures other than the basic business and legal processes, there is little paperwork.

The key process, in stage 4, is about the development of people, they are trusted, and it is only at level four that you can really get the energy, the enthusiasm and the understanding, and motivation of the people involved. At this level the bonus systems are aligned to development of the manager's team and the required culture.

The leadership style is transformational whereby the initiatives come from within.

Organic approach to people development

As the organisation matures up this four level development model, the skills, beliefs and values within the business have to change. It is a process of cultural change and development.

Beliefs and values

The skills of the business go from being a mechanistic type of skill up to developing people. But equally the beliefs and values of the organisation have to change.

At stage 1 there is a belief in submitting claims, a lack of trust between businesses and with the staff, a belief that people do not want to do their best, a belief that this is the way we should run contracts and manage our subcontractors, just through blame and claim.

True belief in the project staff

At stage 4, the beliefs and values have developed. There is a belief about working together, a belief that people want to do their best, a belief that you can get the best out of the project by working together. There is a belief in people, they really believe that people do their best if allowed to and by doing so you are creating trust. So there is a belief in your people and they are fully trusted.

The culture is defined with clear values and the senior management are role models, with the appropriate behaviour reflecting these values.

People's values aligned to the organisational values

Often company values are just stated as separate words e.g. honesty, trust, customer, people. And if they are not linked, the resulting culture becomes less meaningful.

However, if values are linked together in a value statement then they become more powerful.

The values of a business can be separated into:

- Internal values - these reflect the behaviour and attitudes within our own business, and leads to:-
- External values - this reflects the relationship between us and our client that we are striving to achieve
- Client values - this reflects what is valuable to the client, this is the business's reputation

Industries

Different industries are at different levels within this project management development model. Even in the UK, different industries have developed at different rates and levels.

The construction industry in the UK was down at level 1 for a long time. It has been moving to level 2 and level 3.
There are many other industries that are already up to level 3, or 4. These are the mature industries.

Country

The country in which the project is being carried out is also important. There are many cultural differences that have to be considered when appointing a project leader.

If the project leader is appointed to lead a project in a foreign country then the leader has to be fully aware of the culture, of how it works, what behaviour he must adopt to actually influence any people from that country.

A project leader who is working in a foreign country needs to be extremely aware of many of the cultural issues which he has to deal with.

Equally, in different countries, the project management industry may have developed at different stages or rates, and there could be different levels of approach to project management. There are many countries that are at level 1.

Purpose

At level 1, the project purpose would often be to "maximise profit". This could alienate the client and the relationships would be contractual lasting for that project only. In fact the relationship may be damaged by the attitude of the provider thereby making winning work more difficult.

At level 3 and 4, the project purpose would be to create a sustainable profit now and in the future. It would be about creating a sustainable relationship with the client to win more future work, sustainable turnover and profit.

Culture

The effects of business culture can be very damaging on providing the best possible project outcome for a client.

For an example if a leading project management company has statements that they frequently use such as "you must never overrun your task duration" and "you must never be late with your task" and "you must deliver the programme". This implies that the person carrying out the task will be blamed if they overrun or under-run a task.

If this is the case then the person carrying out the task is likely to increase the estimation of their task duration from say 7 days to 10days to allow any for any uncertainties. Also, they are unlikely to report that they have finished early as it would increase pressure on them for the next similar task. They therefore deliver their task on the due date of 10 days even though there was some slack time and they could have finished early, but they didn't.

If this is reflected thoughout the project then the project is inefficient, in this case there is a waste of 43%. But ultimately who pays? The client does.

Client Greater Value, More Profit

As the business develops up this model, far greater value to the client is created. So the client is a lot happier, he becomes less hassled, there are fewer claims, he is more certain of what is going to happen to his project.

On the other hand, the businesses and contractors doing the work will get a lot more profit, because there is less aggravation, there is less wastage, and less time and effort are spent on claims. They are trusted to get on and carry out quality work to time and cost.

As the business develops up this model, focus shifts from a backward looking approach to the project e.g. recovering cost, to a forward looking approach e.g. planning to reduce costs.

**The greater the organisation maturity means the greater
the value to the client and more profit**

So to really achieve the best outcome for your project, the business must be at, if possible, stage 4 where you've got a forward focused vision of what you are going to achieve, and why, and how you are going to achieve it with all of the parties concerned, in complete unity, for mutual benefit.

Development process

It is important that businesses develop along the process, as indicated by the arrows, up the model.

If you are a client that operates at level 3 where you work together, then there is quite a bit of trust and co-operation with those businesses that you work with. Then if a company is employed to do work for you and that company is at level one, then how will this relationship work?

The relationship between those businesses will be strained from the start.
It is very difficult to take on a company that is at level 1 and then immediately change their approach and attitude to match the client's attitude and partnership at level three. A business cannot just change like that. There will need to be a culture change programme, lead by the business's Managing Director, that follows the arrows on this development model.

Also if the client is at stage 1 of the development model, but the business employed to do the work is at stage 3, there will again be tensions and strained relationships. In this case, the project manager must have a strategy of how he will manage the client and possibly get him to move up the maturity model, Fig 2.2.

In reality businesses have to operate at different levels in this model to fit the approach of their clients and other businesses they are working with.

This model is all about the change in the culture, which has to develop of its own accord, and that takes time.

So the relationship between the businesses who are at different levels of maturity is really important in terms of project management and getting the best possible outcome. Unless you get those relationships and culture right, then you will have strain between the businesses concerned, which creates division, tension which wastes time, cost and energy.

To achieve the best possible outcome, where possible, a client and all key businesses involved in a project should have a culture of working together at a similar level, preferably stage 4, focusing together on delivering on what the client wants to achieve.

Need common maturity levels between organisations

So the setting up of long-term relationships is crucial to achieving the best possible outcome.

The purpose of the long-term relationship is to develop together up this maturity model to the ultimate goal of stage 4.

2.5   Organisational Influences

What are the organisational influences on projects?

Often organisations at level 1 are very hierarchal in structure, often with a controlling centre, e.g. head office, with strict job descriptions. These structures become ponderous, slow to changing situations.

Organisations at level 4 are far more flexible and responsive to fast changing environments. They have only loose connections to their centre, have flatter structures and can grow organically.

Functional Organisation

A typical functional organisation is shown in Fig 2.3.

In this case it is made up of a Managing Director, a Board of Directors, and a number of managers heading up departments or functions. The titles may vary with different organisations and different countries.

The organisation's history and structure have a significant bearing on the project performance, particularly if the organisation has been established for a long time, and the structure and attitudes are well entrenched.

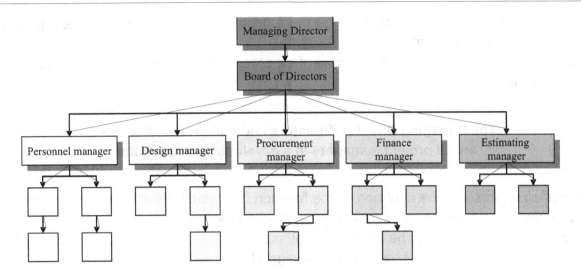

Fig 2.3 Functional Organisation

If the company is developing it should have a clear vision of where it is going and what it has to do in order to achieve that vision and mission. So, clear outcomes will need to be defined.

The type of projects which exist in this type of organisation include:
- The delivery of the vision, and mission with all of the defined strategic outcomes
- Changing the culture and values of the organisation
- Achieving greater profit and turnover
- Acquisition of a new business and the integration of the different cultures
- Developing collaboration with strategic supply chain partners

The project sponsor could be the Managing Director or, for large corporations could be a group board Director.
The project leader could be the Managing Director. The project team could be the Board of Directors, each of whom would be assigned an outcome to achieve.

Each of the functions, headed up by a functional Director, should have their own clear functional outcomes.

Functional projects could include:
- Each function should be managed as a project, providing a defined functional outcome to achieve
- Functional research and development
- Functional implementation of new software
- New functional initiatives
- Supply chain arrangements

The project sponsor in this case will be the functional Director and the project leader would be the functional manager.

The project team would include members of the functional team who have been assigned an outcome

---

The Managing Director, Directors and Functional Managers are all project managers in a developing organisation

---

Specific projects may be confined to the function itself, such as the implementation of new software, achievement of new targets or outcomes.

The project sponsor could be the functional manager.

The project manager could be a person assigned from within the function.

- o Achievement of new functional targets
- o Achievement of the functional process objectives
- o Process re-engineering within the function
- o 6 Sigma improvement targets

The project sponsor is likely to be the functional manager, the project leader will be a functional team member who has been assigned an outcome

---

The developing organisation and all functions are projects

Many developing organisations do not recognise that they could achieve their desired results using a project management approach. If they do, then they are more likely to be far more profitable.

Single project organisations

This type of organisation is shown in Fig 2.4

In addition to the functional organisation, within the head office, with all the different types of project, as described above, this organisation also has a specific single project.

The one-off specific project, like this, could including
- o research and development
- o implementing major new software
- o building
- o construction
- o different phases of a complex project (e.g. feasibility, design, setting up, steady state, commissioning and closing down)

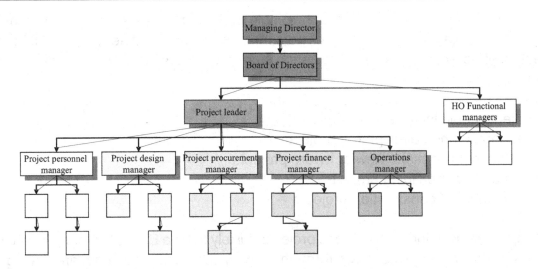

Fig 2.4 Single Project Organisation

The project sponsor is likely to be a Board Director.

The project leader reports directly to the Board through his sponsor and has specific outcomes to deliver.

The project team are managers of their specialist project based functions and operations, and are assigned their outcomes.

The project leader of a single project is all powerful

The tensions here are that the project leader has full authority over his team. So there may be little contact between the project's functions and the head office's functions. In some cases, the project's functions may have developed approaches/processes that could be completely different to the HO functions.

Multi-single project organisations

This type of organisation is shown in Fig 2.5 below.

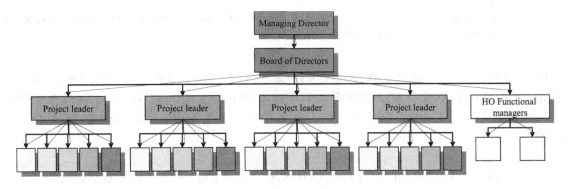

Fig 2.5 Multi-Single Project Organisation

This type of organisation is similar to the single project organisation but with a number of significant projects. There is little or no contact between the different projects. Each project is effectively managed in isolation from the others with all the project team reporting to the project leader.

The projects could include
- o research and development projects
- o implementing major new software projects
- o a number of building projects
- o a number of construction projects

The project sponsor, for each of these projects is likely to be a Board Director, the project leader reports directly to the Board through his sponsor, the project team are managers of their specific project based functions, and are assigned their outcomes.

The project leaders are all powerful in single or multi-project environments

---

The tensions here are that again the project leader is powerful with full authority over his team. So there is little or no contact between the projects or between the project's functions and the HO functions. So different systems could be developed on different projects thereby duplicating effort.

However, the project leader would want to maintain his complete authority and therefore not necessarily allow a team member to be part of a separate development team.

A key question is how to ensure the balance between centralisation and non-centralisation of systems and approaches. On the one hand it is important to ensure creativity and innovation on projects, but also to reduce waste and duplication by having common systems. Imposing too much "control" from centre could inhibit creativity and lower morale on projects and split responsibilities/authority between the project ands the HO.

For example, if there are a number of large projects, located miles away from the HO, and there is a central buying team based in HO for the procurement of all products and services for all the different projects.

The HO buying team may have different priorities to your project, in that they are busy buying for another project and hence the buying of your product, which may be a result of an urgent change, may get delayed and this could well easily delay your project overall.

Then who is responsible for the product delivery and the delays to the project?

This waters-down the project leader's authority for performance, their hands appear to be constrained.

There needs to be a balance between central buying and the need for "economies of scale", and the need for projects to be "flexible" to meet the changing needs of the client, market and project.

Another key question is the portfolio of projects and getting the right balance of projects for the organisation that suits the organisation's strategies, business plan and core competencies.

Multi-project organisation

This type of organisation is shown in Fig 2.6

In addition to the functional organisation, made up of many projects. The resources are shared across the projects.

The projects in this case could include:
- Design office with a multitude of designs sharing design resource
- Cross-functional development or improvements

For each of the specific projects the project sponsor is likely to be a Board Director, the project leader reports directly to the Board through his sponsor. The project team are shared between different projects and have different project outcomes.

The difficulty with this type of organisation is that the resources are shared across the projects. There are no project teams dedicated solely to a single project. This causes tension between the project leaders. Which is the priority project for the team member to work on? Of course each project leader will insist that their project is the most important, but this may not be the case. The resources will normally respond to the project leader that they know, or have worked with before, or the project leader who shouts the loudest.

The project leaders share power in multi-project organisations

---

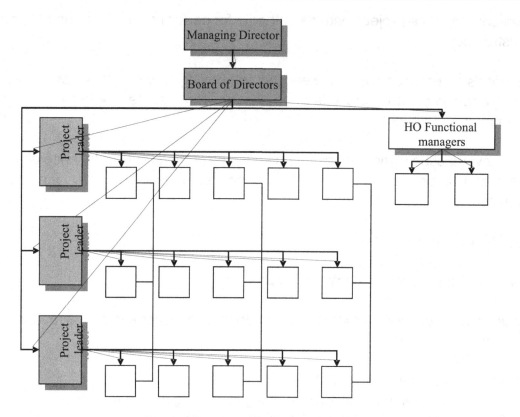

Fig 2.6 Multi-project organisation

The project leader is not all powerful. It is very difficult for any project leader to be truly effective in this type of organisation. The leader spends a lot of his time managing and negotiating the resource time and coercing them to work on his project, so frustrations and inefficiencies creep in.

Matrix type organisation

The matrix type organisation is shown in Fig 2.7

It is the hardest type of organisation in which to manage a project. Here, the project team comprises members of existing functions.

The projects in this case could include:
  o Design office with a multitude of designs sharing design resource
  o Design and construction
  o Cross-functional development or improvements

For each of the specific projects the project sponsor could be a Board Director, or it could be a functional manager. The project leader reports directly to the project sponsor.

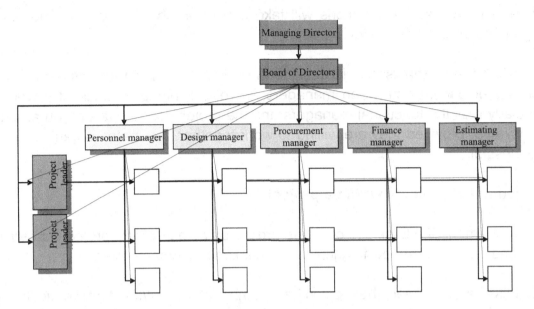

Fig 2.7 Matrix type of organisation

The project members are made up of people from existing functional teams and have dual responsibilities to both the functional manager and to the project manager with different outcomes.

A lot of tension can result from this arrangement, especially if the functional arrangements have been in place for a very long time with experienced managers heading them.

If the Board of directors decides that a project is required to achieve a particular outcome or result, and they appoint a young enthusiastic project leader. He is going to struggle as he will have no authority over the functional managers and he has to coerce agreements for their staff to spend time on the project. The functional managers may or not co-operate with the young project leader, depending on his own pressures and relationships.

So the project leader has very little authority.

Managing Director leads change in culture to a project management approach

In some cases a special committee has to be appointed to manage the portfolio of projects and the resources over the heads of the project leader and the functional managers.

An example of this could be a local government organisation with a long history of engrained attitudes in a functional hierarchy. Bringing in a project management type arrangements across the functions will take a considerable amount of time, and a change of culture, led by the top person.

If a newly formed organisation is designed in a matrix format then, as there will be no history or baggage between managers, there is a higher chance of it working. Particularly if all the functional managers and the project leader start off on an equal authority and, provided they are willing to work together, the matrix organisation can be successful.

Management of projects within a project

The management of a business could be organised as a strategic project achieving a vision, and mission with new financial results, takeovers and mergers.

Within this strategic project there could be a number of tactical/functional projects each operating as a project. Each function should have its own outcome/vision and purpose/ mission.

Within these functions there could be many operational projects.

The organisation could be managed as a single strategic project which includes a number of tactical projects, each one including a number of operational projects.

Also the organisation could include single projects which, within themselves, may have sub-projects.

This is a cascade from a single strategic project, to many projects, to a multitude of projects within the organisation. If all these projects are aligned and delivered, this will enhance organisational performance considerably, Fig 2.8.

All these strategic, tactical, and operational projects must have:
- Clear outcome/vision
- Clear reason/purpose/mission
- Clear logical diagram
- Defined their clients/customers needs and values
- Have the right project leader responsible for achieving the project outcome, purpose
- Have a timescale
- Have a budget
- Have a project team

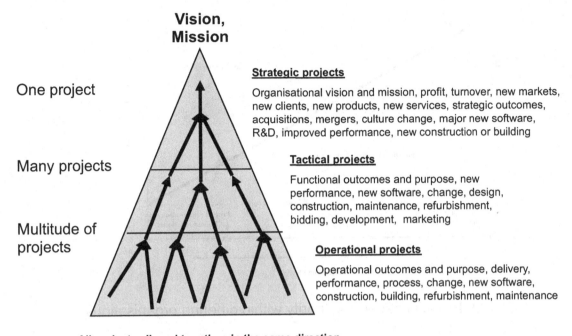

All projects aligned together, in the same direction

Fig 2.8 Cascade of projects within a strategic project to achieve a vision

This applies at all levels in the organisation, this is the management of projects within a project.

2.6   Project Leader's Organisational Authority

The level of authority, that the project leader has, very much depends upon the type of organisation within which the project is being managed.

The diagram below, Fig 2.9, links the authority of the project leader to the organisational type and also the complexity of project.

The project leader's competency and the tensions of running the project will depend on where the organisation is on this diagram

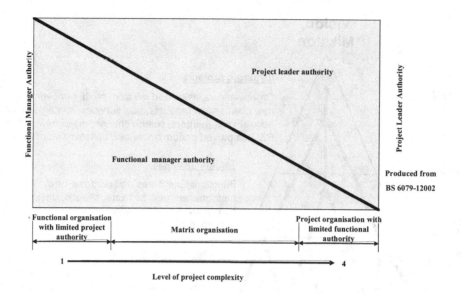

Fig 2.9 Project Leader's Authority within differing organisations

Type of project leader must be appropriate to the project type, size and complexity

The more complex the project, the greater the required competency level of the project leader, and the greater the authority that he will need to have in order to execute the project most effectively, Fig 2.10

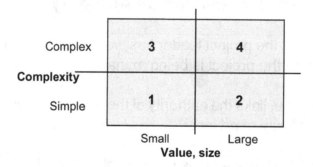

Fig 2.10 Project complexity, size grid

The following diagram, Fig 2.11, relates the competency level to the complexity of the project, 1-4, Fig 2.10, with level 5 being the management of a portfolio programme of projects. Also the type of training and knowledge that the project leader requires is indicated.

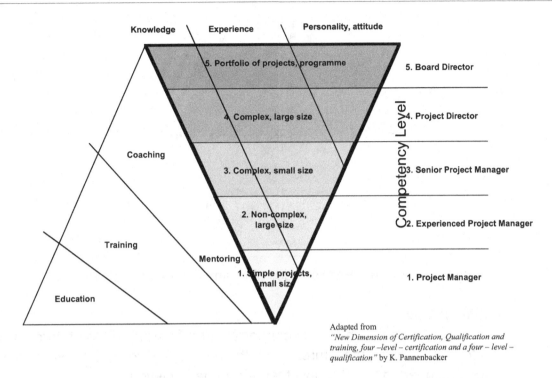

Fig 2.11 Project leader's competency and project complexity

**Project leader's competency and experience levels
reflect the project's size and complexity**

2.7   Personality of project leader

The personality style of the project leader is essential for ensuring the best possible outcome. If the wrong leader is appointed at the start of the project, it will set off on the wrong footing. And, once it has done this and gone down a set route, it is really difficult to recover that situation.

So it is really important to plan to have the right project leader at the start for the type of project, the size and complexity, and recognising the various stages of maturity of the businesses involved.

Personal Profile

People have different approaches and personality styles. These styles are appropriate for different project types and roles within projects, and can be determined quickly and easily. There are many profiling techniques but the technique that is particularly useful and identifies the role of the project leader, Fig 2.12, refer to www.projectmanagementbusiness. com

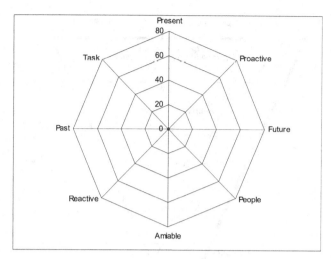

Fig 2.12 Personal Profile radar diagram (after Dan Patey)

o Future orientated
   This type of person is naturally comfortable on focusing on the future. He is comfortable defining the future, where the business is going to be, what those outcomes need to be, and how they are to be achieved.

o Present orientated
   This type of person thinks mainly about what is happening today, next week, or this next month. They are reactive, something has to be done now—they are task driven. These people are very good at being reactive to whatever comes up, and are able to organise and achieve the work and tasks that needs to be done this week or next week.

o Past orientated
   There are many people who are only focused on the past, they can only think of what's happened previously, following the past process. They are comfortable with this, with the way things were done in the past, and they are happy to continue doing things in exactly the same way.

   e.g. design work is carried out using very similar processes and systems. Past orientated people like running with the same processes which has been developed that they fully understand. They only focus on doing what they are comfortable with.

o Amiable orientated
   Many people try to satisfy others, they are just amiable, they just do as they are told, they like to help others. They are not that good at planning or programming or looking to the future, and are not task driven.

Different project types and sizes will require different type of person leading or managing the project. The type of personality of the project leader must depend on the complexity and size of the project.

The project leader's personality matches the required role profile

For a complex project all of these characteristics will be required within the senior team.

Direction, Navigation, Destination, Action (DNDA) Profile

Another aspect of the project leader's profile and personality is their natural preference for focusing on one of the following, Fig 2.13.

- o Direction or purpose
  Some people are driven by purpose, the reason why they are doing things.

- o Destination or vision, outcomes
  Some people like to focus on the outcome, or a vision (a vision is just a large long-term outcome). They like to clearly define outcomes. They often like to develop concepts and focus on them.

- o Navigation, planning
  There are some people who enjoy getting into the detail of planning.

- o Action
  Other people just like taking action.

If you have a project leader who is driven by purpose to achieve the future, then that is probably the best profile for a leader of a complex project.

If you have someone who is driven by purpose for the present, they have the ability to drive a short or medium project forward to achieve results. Many projects leaders are like this.

Some people just like to take action, these people would be good running small short-term task orientated project, where they may be doing the work themselves.

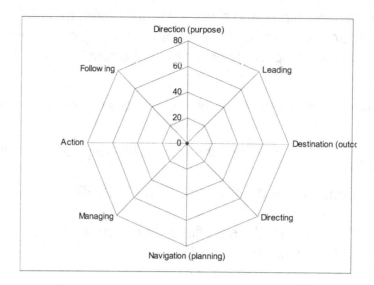

Fig 2.13 Business Profile radar diagram (DNDA)

The personality of the project leader must depend upon the type and complexity of the project, the culture and development stages of the industry and country within which the project is being carried out.

Complex projects

The future and purpose orientated leader is really important for complex projects where new systems, a new approach, and understanding have to be developed to complete the project. He has new outcomes to achieve, things that he has never done before.

The future and purpose orientated project leader need to be comfortable having that clarity and vision, but he has to communicate that to his senior team and other project staff.

Complex project require future orientated leaders

On a complex project the project leader needs all personality types on his team, the present focused persons to achieve results, the past focused people to operate the existing systems well, and the amiable focused people to help others use the systems.

Simple Project

Simple projects will be carried out using existing systems and processes. There will be no need to develop new ways, as the project will be similar to many others, with straightforward task to do. A past or present oriented project leader could be appropriate.

Simple projects require past or present orientated leaders

Some examples of these type of profiles for a project leader are as follows.

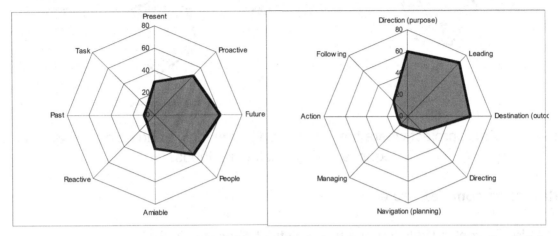

Fig 2.14 Complex project where the leader is leading (purpose and outcome) to achieve the future, develops new ways

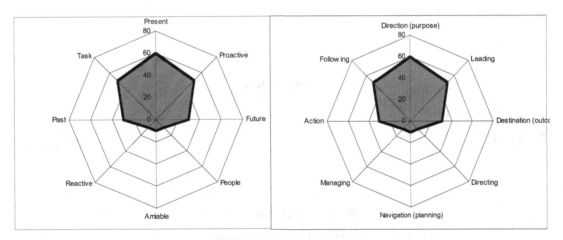

Fig 2.15 Medium sized project where the leader is focused on purpose for the present, just getting things done this week and month

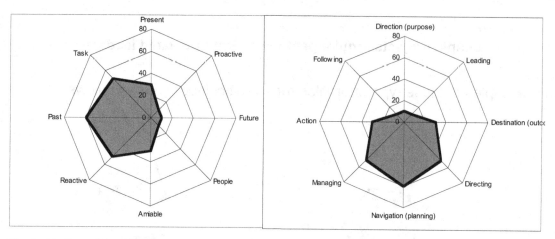

Fig 2.16 Small project where the focus is on just planning and doing the task, as required, using existing methods

Setting up a complex project

A complex project is likely to have three distinct phases, Fig 2.17.
1. Initial setting up phase.
2. Steady state
3. Final closing down phase

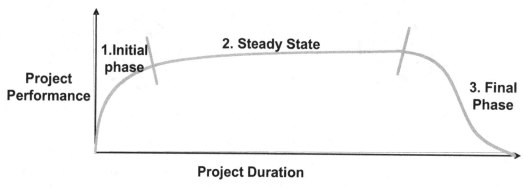

Fig 2.17 Project phases

When a large complex project is being set up—developing new ways, new approaches, new systems, new processes, and new relationships—the project staff have to be trained in their role until a steady state is achieved.

A future orientated leader would be required to clearly define what has to be done, and provide direction. When a steady state has been achieved, the leader could be changed to a present focused leader, one who "turns the handle" of the now defined systems and processes and makes them work.

There may need to be different project leaders with different personalities for different phases of a complex project. These include: feasibility, planning, start up and the setting up, running and then the closing down.

Each of these phases is a project in itself, and may be best to have different leaders with different personalities to carry out each one.

Different project leaders may be best for different project phases

---

Often project leaders have managed all these phases of performance even though they may be good at only one phase but not necessarily good at all of them. We should be able to change project leaders by recognising their strengths and aligning them and their characteristics to the needs of that project phase.

If we have the right personality for the type, size and phase of the project, then we are going to start the project with the best chance of getting the best possible outcome.

Chapter 2—Project Context

What have you discovered about project management?

How can you apply this to your projects?

What ideas has it given you to improve your project management?

What are some actions you can take to start managing your projects to achieve the best possible outcome?

1.

2.

3.

4.

5.

The Best Project Strategy

3   The Best Project Strategy

When a project does not fully deliver, then where does it normally fail? It normally fails at the start of the project and not at the end.

3.1   Strategic Thinking

In order to achieve the best possible outcome one has to start with the strategic thinking for the project. The clearer this is the greater the chances of achieve the desired project outcome.

If the project team is not clear as to what the project is trying to achieve and what their role is, then there may be confusion, wastage and the project will not achieve the best outcome.

This section is about defining that strategic thinking, and the strategic plan, to produce the best project strategy.

The Best Strategic Thinking

This can be applied to both simple and complex projects. The principles are the same, but different levels of thinking and complexity are required. So what are the key elements of strategic thinking? To do this we will consider the Business Journey.

3.2   The Business Journey

All developing businesses are on a journey, otherwise they would not be developing. Any strategic thinking is taking the business on a journey which aims to achieve a new result or outcome.

The following diagram, Fig 3.1, compares a business to a journey from London to Edinburgh. The elements of this journey are:

1. The purpose, mission for the journey
2. The problem that the business is trying to overcome
3. The vision, outcome or destination of where we want to get to
4. The strategy and mode of transport, which has time and cost implications
5. The timescale to achieve the outcome
6. The responsibilities of who does what
7. The risks that prevent us achieving the outcome
8. The costs and budget for the journey
9. The monitoring achievement of the journey to time and cost
10. The culture and values, working together

The Business Journey
Strategic Thinking

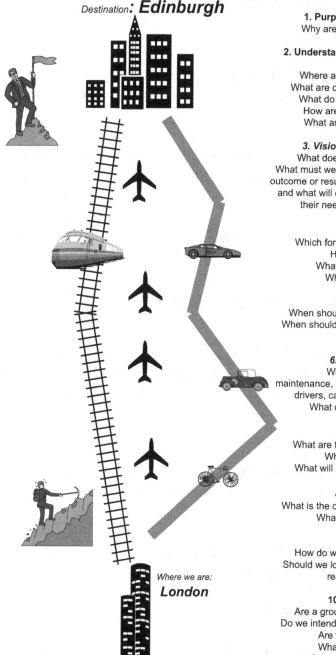

1. Purpose (Mission), direction:
Why are we going on this journey?

2. Understanding Ourselves, problem to overcome
Where are we now? What is it like?
What are our strengths & weaknesses?
What do our customers think of us?
How are we perceived by others?
What are we trying to overcome?

3. Vision, outcome, destination:
What does our destination look like?
What must we achieve? What are the required outcome or results? What will it look like, feel like and what will our stakeholders say? What are their needs? What is success like?

4. Strategy
Which form of transport will we take?
How fast will we go?
What route are we to take?
What is the road map?

5. Timescale
When should we reach our destination?
When should we arrive at key points on the journey?

6. Responsibilities:
Who should look after
maintenance, refreshments, hotels, training of drivers, cash for journey, navigation?
What do we need to achieve?

7. Risks
What are the obstacles to overcome?
What could go wrong?
What will stop us from getting there?

8. Costs, budget
What is the cost or budget for the journey?
What is the spend profile?

9. Monitoring:
How do we know we are on course?
Should we look at speed, mileage, time of reaching landmarks?

10. Culture, values:
Are a group of us to travel together?
Do we intend arriving all at the same time?
Are we in separate cars?
What are we capable of?
Do we coach each other on:-
the route; the speed of travel; refreshment stops; mechanical difficulties; health requirements?
How do we behave to each other?

Fig 3.1 The Business Journey

If a business can define where it wants to get to, its vision, and why, then this is a journey, but it is also a project. Managing a developing business, achieving its vision and mission, is a project and can be managed using project management techniques.

3.3   The 4 Questions of Project Management (4Qs)

We have found that many businesses and projects do not deliver their full potential. This is often because the business, and its projects and sub-projects, have not been defined sufficiently at the start.

It is essential for the following questions, 4Qs, to be answered.
Q1. What must the project have achieved? - outcome.
Q2. Why must we have achieved this outcome now? - purpose
Q3. What problem must the project overcome? Or what opportunity is there?
Q4. What must we have done to achieve the outcome? - logical diagram

Q1, Q2, Q3 should be defined by the project owner/sponsor. The logical diagram, Q4, should be defined by the project team.

The 4Qs provide the clarity and direction for the project. Without clear answers to these questions then the project cannot deliver the best possible outcome for your client.

Since a business is a project then the 4Qs can be applied at all levels, strategic, tactical and also operational.

Define the 4Qs for all aspects of running your business

Q1 Project Outcome

What is the project outcome?
What is the change in business performance that will result from the project? What is the performance outcome or result that has to be achieved?

This definition has to be absolutely clear and unambiguous.

This is the *outcome* of the project that the project manager and his team must deliver. It must not be confused with output or objective. It is a change in business performance or result.

Ideally it is a statement written in past tense as if it has already been achieved, but has not yet been achieved. It must be easily measured.

The benefits to the business when the outcome of a project is achieved should be defined,

Current difficulties

Often projects are not clear in their outcome. If so then how can the project staff achieve an outcome that has not been clearly defined? And how can we expect them to be effective?

As people often want to do their best, and if the outcome and reason is not clear, then they will adopt a role and their own direction, which they believe is appropriate. They may be pointing in a slightly wrong direction, and if this happens with all the key personnel across the project then this creates tensions, differences, waste and inefficiencies.

All this adds up to increased costs, becoming uncompetitive, with reduced market share.

Clarity of project outcome

Without this clarity at the start of the project then the best possible outcome cannot be achieved.

As Covey S.R. (1999) says start with the end in mind.

Clarity of project vision, or outcome, destination

The outcome of the project should be the required change or improvement in performance which in turn provides the benefit and return on investment.

The outcome is what the PM and his team are required to achieve at the end of the project.

Q2 Purpose, mission, why

Why is this project outcome important to your client, why is it being carried out? Why must the outcome be achieved and why by a stated date? This is the mission, aim, intent or the purpose of the project. The purpose is the driving force for the project staff.

The purpose, mission, aim, of your project, provides direction.

Also, why is this project important to your business? This could give a different perspective in why your business needs to deliver a successful project for your client.

Also why is this project important to you as the PM? This is your own personal purpose and provides the reason why you are managing this project, your own personal motivation.

This provides the direction that we are pointing in. If the purpose has not been defined then the business will be going round in circles. It will have no compass or bearing by which to steer.

When the staff say that there is "no direction", they are meaning that there is no purpose or reason why they have to do something. It is the purpose that provides the direction.

If your project has a compelling purpose, and all your staff are aligned to that purpose, then you are far more likely to achieve the required exceptional performance. Without this definition then only mediocre results can be achieved.

Without a defined purpose then your staff will not be fully motivated since purpose provides motivation.

Reason why/purpose/aim = Motive/motivation

Q3 Overcoming a problem or achieveing an opportunity

What is the problem that this project is trying to overcome or what is the opportunity?

A project is a change to something. And a change is a solution to something, and all solutions overcome problems. Therefore, all projects overcome problems. The problem that the project is overcoming must be clearly defined and should be performance related.

Define the problem and opportunity

It is only when the problem is defined that alternative approaches can be considered.

Too often the solution, or project outcome, has been totally inappropriate. This is because the problem that they were trying to overcome had not been clearly identified. If it had, then a different and more effective solution would have been found and implemented.

The problem that the project aims to overcoming must be clearly stated.

Alternatively there may be an opportunity in the market [pace for a client. So the project is set up to exploit that opportunity, but the client's purpose needs still to be defined.

Q4 Logical Diagram

Once the project outcome and purpose have been stated then the logical diagram has to be defined. This is what must be achieved that, if completed, will actually deliver the project outcome? These are the "what statements" or sub-outcomes.

The logical diagram is not a "pert" diagram from a gantt chart as the thought process is different.

When constructing this logical diagram, from the already defined Q1, Q2, Q3, the representatives of the team need to be involved

- o this defines everything that must be in place that, collectively, will ensure the outcome is achieved.
- o arrange these statements, working back from the outcome, in logical "must have" order.
- o these are sub-outcomes.

Check that the logic is correct reading back from the outcome, Fig 3.2.

in order to achieve "O", I must have "C" and "G"
in order to achieve "C", I must have "B"
in order to achieve "B", I must have "A"
in order to achieve "G", I must have "E" and "F"
in order to achieve "E", I must have "D"
in order to achieve "F", I must have "D"

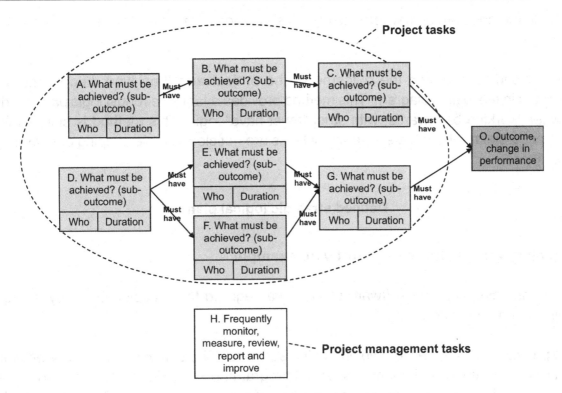

Fig 3.2 Logical diagram

It is important that each sub-outcome statement on the diagram is clear. The tense is important. If the action is a one-off action then the statement must be in the past tense as if it has already been completed. For the establishment of an on-going process then the statement can be in the present tense. By doing this it is easy to confirm whether the action has been completed or not.

When the logic has been established for the whole diagram, the person responsible for achieving each sub-outcome is identified. They define how long they will take to complete their sub-outcome, this is the duration of effort and not elapsed time.

It is important that the people responsible are involved with this exercise, as they have to take the actions and they need to understand and agree what the logical diagram is.

They need to understand the 4Qs for their project, the logical diagram, and how they fit into it. They will "get" the big picture and are more likely to "buy-into" it.

There are two approaches to constructing the logic of a project programme.

The first, forward thinking, from where we are in the logical sequence of the construction of the programme, then defining what the next task is, progressively working forward until the programme is completed with the completion of the project. This may be suitable for those projects where the logical sequence of tasks is clear e.g. constructing a house.

The second is to define the outcome of the project and then work backwards, as indicated in the logical diagram. This method provides a far more robust logic particularly if, when working backwards, with strict "must have" logic. This method is suitable for abstract projects where the sequence of tasks are not clear e.g. developing or changing a business.

Defined strategic logical plan

Objective versus Outcome—Software example

A new process mapping software product was agreed to be implemented by a large multi-million pound company.

The project objective was to "implement the software". The software had been identified and it was agreed to implement it. A roll out programme was produced and the software was installed. But what does "implement the software" actually mean? In this example the software was installed, people trained, and their processes mapped. So you could say the objective had been met, Fig 3.3.

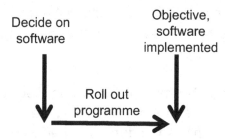

Decide on software

Objective, software implemented

Roll out programme

Fig 3.3 Software implementation not linked into business performance

But there was no improvement to the business performance with this statement. As a result there was no improved business performance. In fact since there was considerable cost involved with the implementation, the profitability of the business took a serious hit.

Too often the project does not lead to a change in performance as a result of the implementation of the software.

Therefore the benefits that could be achieved were not.

What should have happened? If the 4Qs of PM had been defined and the logical diagram had been implemented, then it would have been highly likely that the outcome and purpose would have been achieved and the benefit of the project realised, Fig 3.4.

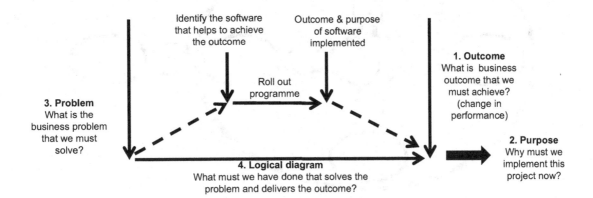

Fig 3.4 Software implementation linked into business performance

The software is a mechanism that helps to achieve the change in performance, and the change in business performance should be the outcome of the project and not the objective of installation of the software.

3.4   Stakeholder's needs

Who are the key stakeholders and what are their needs? What will make them say that the project was a success?

The project staff have to understand and satisfy the stakeholders' needs, these include both their the corporate needs and their emotional needs of the person representing that business.

Stakeholder definition

What do we mean by stakeholder?

A key stakeholder is someone, or a group, who have a significant influence on the outcome of a project. That person could either be internal or external to the project.

The following diagram, Fig 3.5, identifies the six stakeholder categories.

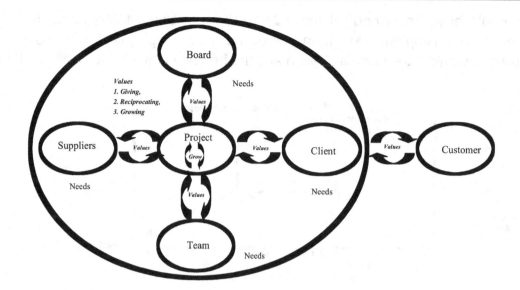

Fig 3.5 Stakeholder categories

These six categories include:
- The client
  - These are key decision makers, they pay for the project, they need regular updates, and the project leader comes into regular contact with them
- The client's customer
  - These are the customers of the client who will be using the project's product or service
  - May include interest groups that could affect the project outcome and purpose
- The company Board
  - These include the Project Leader's Manager or Director
- The supply chain
  - These businesses that provide the project with products or services
- The project team
  - The staff reporting directly to the project leader
- The project leader
  - The project leader himself

Key stakeholders

The stakeholders can be grouped into four categories, as shown in Fig 3.6

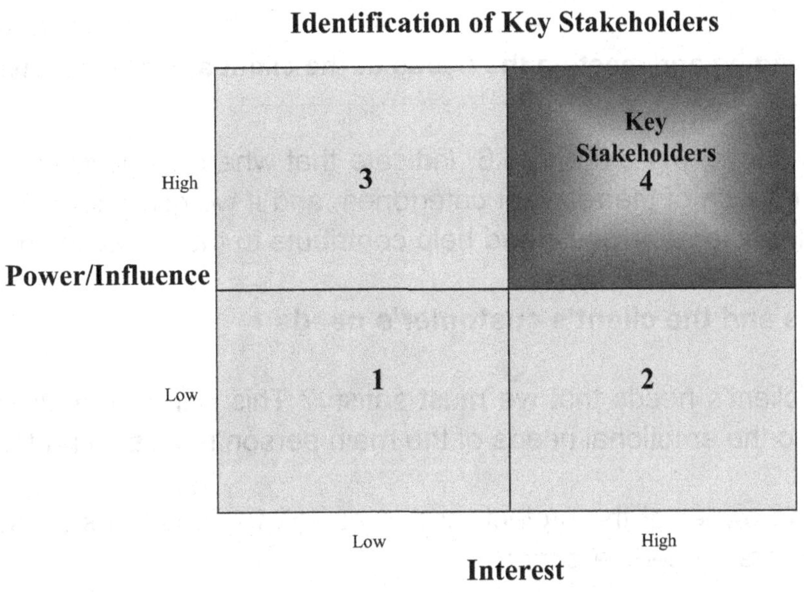

Identification of Key Stakeholders

Fig 3.6 Power/interest analysis for key stakeholders

Within each of these categories, there will be key individuals with the potential to influence the project outcome, group 4. These individuals, or key stakeholders, will have to be identified and named. Each of these groups have a different degree of interest and potential to influence, so each group will have to be managed differently.

Define key stakeholders

Group 1 could be ignored since they have low interest and low influence on the project. Group 2 and 3 may need to be managed depending on the individual persons and their role. But group 4, the key stakeholders, will need to be managed as they will have a huge impact on the project's success. A stakeholder plan will have to be developed that manages these people.

This power/interest analysis, for the key stakeholders, should be applied to each of the categories:
- Client
- Client's customers
- Company Board
- Supply chain
- Project Team

This analysis will give the project leader a good idea of the most important people that he must concentrate on.

Understanding and meeting the needs of the client and client's customers

The diagrams above, Fig 3.5 and 3.6, indicate that when we have identified our key stakeholders, in each of the relevant categories, and if we give them what they need, then they are likely to reciprocate and help contribute to the project's success.

Client's needs and the client's customer's needs

What are the client's needs that we must satisfy? This will be the client's corporate needs, and also the emotional needs of the main person representing the client.

The client is the owner of the project, and is paying for it. He has to ensure that his company's corporate needs are met.

The corporate needs of the client are likely to be:
- o achievement of the project outcome, purpose, the results, the benefits
- o to be successful and to be seen to be successful
- o delivery on time
- o delivery to cost
- o delivery of the required quality or standard
- o satisfying key customers

The client will have some personal emotional needs which will reassure him that the project is running on time and his corporate needs will be achieved. Fig 3.7 gives an indication of what these emotional needs may be.

The client must also consider his own customers' needs. These customers could include members of the public, Members of Parliament, or members of splinter or specialist groups. They could all have a major influence on the project. The client's needs are influenced by their own customers' needs.
If the client's needs are being met then he is likely to enthusiastically promote the project.

However, in order for the client to trust the project leader, the project leader has to earn that trust, he has to do what he has promised, he has to listen and to really understand the client and to do what the client wants him to do within the contractual boundaries.

Trust will then be earned and the project will then "grow" as a success in the eyes of the client.

6 emotional needs	The client must believe:
Certainty	1. in the abilities of the project leader, and the project team to achieve the outcome 2. that he is kept updated with the project performance and any potential difficulties or overruns 3. that everything is being done by the project leader and the team to achieve the best possible outcome
Choice	1. that he has the ability to make the right decisions for his business 2. that the project leader will involve him with any key decisions that affects the project's outcome
Significance	1. that his position is important for the success of the project 2. that the project leader will involve him
Connection, Rapport	1. that he will get on well with the project leader 2. that the project leader listens to and understands his concerns
Growth	1. that he can learn about the issues that the project leader has 2. that he can understand more about the project
Contribution	1. that he can contribute to the project's success in achieving the best possible outcome 2. that he contributes to his own business's success

Fig 3.7 Client's emotional needs

These 6 emotional needs, certainty, choice, significance, connection, growth, contribution, can be applied to all the key stakeholders

The key to success is to get the client to promote the project to his own Director and other influential people in his business. To do this the project leader must demonstrate that everything is being done to bring the project in on time, to cost and to standard.

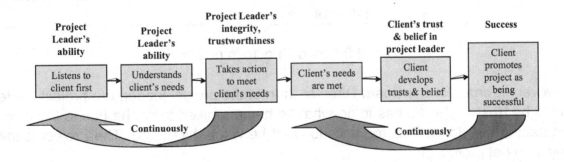

Fig 3.8 Client promoting the project, hence success

Corporate Company—Board Director's needs

This is the internal part of the project leader's business, the Board Director, or manager, that the project leader reports to. The corporate needs could include:

- o complying with legislation e.g. health and safety, environment
- o achieving the required profit and turnover
- o enhancing the company's reputation and repeat work

The Board Director, to whom the project leader reports, will have his own personal emotional needs that will give him confidence that the project will met his corporate needs.

Possible examples of these are included in the table, Fig 3.9, however the project leader must make his own list that reflects the actual people he is dealing with.

	The Board Director must believe:
Certainty	1. that the corporate needs will be met 2. that he is kept updated with regular, timely information of project performance and likely outcome 3. that there are no surprises
Choice	1. that the project leader would involve him in the key decisions that may affect the project performance
Significance	1. that the project leader listens to him and understands his views, and takes action
Connection, Rapport	1. that there is good relationship with the project leader 2. there is openness and support
Growth	1. that the project helps the company to grow and learn 2. the success of the project helps the Board Director to be in good favour
Contribution	1. that the project contributes to the profit, increased market share and reputation of the company

Fig 3.9 Board Director's needs

However, in order for the Board Director to trust the project leader, the project leader has to be trustworthy, he has to do what he has promised to do, he has to listen and understand the Board Director, and do what he wants him to do. The project leader may then get promotion.

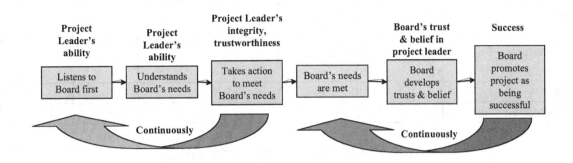

Fig 3.10 Board promoting the project—hence success

The role of the project leader is to ensure that the needs of the client and his Board Director are fully met. This is done by listening, understanding and taking action, Fig 3.10.

By doing so trust will develop and the project will be seen as successful in the eyes of the client and also the Board Director. This perception of success is important.

Key Stakeholder Satisfaction

Having understood who the key stakeholders are, their six emotional needs and the importance of managing those needs, the project leader has to manage them.

A judgement can then be made of how well these needs are being met. The table below, Fig 3.11, is an example of how to score this.

This scoring can be the project leader's own assessment, but it would be better from the client.

6 emotional needs	Client's needs:	Score				
		Strongly disagree	Disagree	Neutral	Agree	Strongly agree
		0	1	2	3	4
Certainty	1. 2.					
Choice	1. 2.					
Significance	1. 2.					
Connection, Rapport	1. 2.					

Growth	1.					
	2.					
Contribution	1.					
	2.					
Total						
Percentage						

Fig 3.11 Key stakeholders score sheet

From this scoring sheet, a radar diagram, Fig 3.12, can be produced and the weaknesses will be highlighted, and actions can be identified and implemented. The target would be to score 80% in meeting all of the clients needs.

If any one of these needs are not achieved then they will not promote the project.

This type of survey could be used for all of the key stakeholders, and from this an action plan can be produced to improve the score and hence satisfy them.

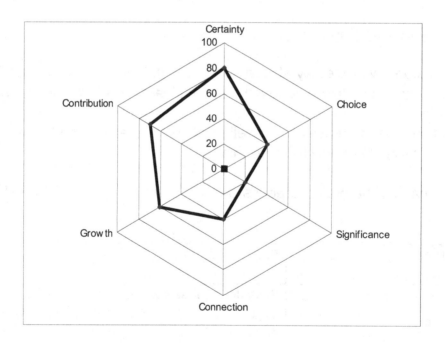

Fig 3.12 Diagram of the Client's emotional needs survey

3.5   Definition of Success

The definition of success of the project has to be from the perspective of the client and sponsor with answers to the following:

What is the project scope, deliverables and definition of success of the project?

What are we expecting to have completed?
What will success look like?
What will the key stakeholders say about the project?
What will it feel like having completed the project?
What are the benefits having completed the project?

In order for a project to be successful, the client and the Board Director have to actively promote it. It is their perception that determines success of the project.

Defined success criteria

The success criteria need to be listed from the viewpoint of the client and the Board Director.

This is likely to include:
- o actual performance to time, budget, standard
- o safety, environmental issues
- o client satisfaction, needs met
- o customer satisfaction
- o board satisfaction, needs met
- o project leader's ability and professionalism
- o project team's and supply chain's effectiveness and professionalism
- o culture and attitude and motivation
- o good communication and relationships with the Client, no surprises

---

The perception of success by the Client and Board Director is key to success

---

3.6   Detailed Programme

The logical diagram is converted into a detailed programme. Each of the sub-outcomes statements in the logical diagram becomes a roll up bar in the programme with a number of defined tasks that will achieve each of the sub-outcomes.

These tasks should:
- o Be stated in the past tense since it is easier to know when they are completed
- o All tasks must be logically linked with their predecessors and successors
- o Durations that reflect the amount of effort, not elapsed time
- o Persons defined who are responsible for each task

There may be some activities that should not appear on the detailed programme as they would likely confuse the logic. For example any regular reviews, meetings to check progress and financial performance. These activities can be outlined within the project strategy document.

3.7   Measures

What measures will determine the success of the project?
These measures must be directly linked to the project outcome and the logical diagram.

Key Performance Indicators (KPIs)

In the UK there has been a surge of interest in KPIs. Everything has to be measured, and in order to manage something, it must be measured.

However there is a big danger with KPIs.

It has been long accepted that people's behaviour is related to the way they are measured. If this is the case, and if the KPIs do not link up to the desired outcome, then the wrong behaviours will be created, which won't be aligned to the desired outcome and the project will not deliver its potential.

People behave the way they are measured

If there are a plethora of KPIs not linked to the desired outcomes, they will be creating a business in which staff will be aligned in slightly different directions. This creates a very weak business without any clear direction.

If the business is to be dynamic, fast moving and fast changing, then there has to be only one overall outcome and a series of cascaded sub-outcomes. There should be only one corresponding measure reflecting the overall outcome, and a cascade of measures reflecting the cascade of sub-outcomes.

By doing this, the outcomes will be aligned, the KPIs will be aligned, and the people will be aligned.

First of all define the overall outcome, and purpose, then the logical diagram which defines the other sub-outcomes, then define the measures and KPIs that demonstrate the achievement of the logical diagram.

Project outcome measure

The outcome of the project must be stated in a way that can be measured.

If the outcome is complex, i.e. it has a number of elements, all of these elements must be achieved together for the project to be successful. Therefore there is still only one measure for the project outcome, it may be as simple as a confirmation that the outcome, with all its constituents parts, was achieved.

Logical diagram measures

Each of the "what must be achieved" sub-outcomes statements must be stated in such a way that they can be measured. The measure may be as simple as a confirmation that these statements have been achieved.

Defined measures linked to achieving the outcome and logical plan

---

3.8   Timescale

What is the overall timescale? When should the outcome and sub-outcomes of the project be completed?

The timescale for the overall completion must be clear. When defined, and since all the durations on the logical plan have been produced, then the start date of the project can be determined with a clear reason why.

Defined timescale to achieve the outcome and logical plan

3.9   Responsibilities

What are the roles and responsibilities of the key people? What are their own outcomes and purpose, linked into the logical diagram?

These include:
- o   project sponsor, Board Director
- o   project leader
- o   project team

Responsibilities for delivering each of the sub-outcomes on the logical plan must be defined. The project leader has overall responsibilities for the delivery of the logical diagram and the project outcome by the required date. The Board Director's role should also be defined to ensure there are clear boundaries of their involvement.

Responsibilities may include different companies if the project is a joint venture.

The project team's responsibilities, role and outcome, are defined in the logical diagram. These may be developed into job descriptions but must be linked back to the logical diagram and detailed programme. Each role must have its own purpose.

If the project is large and complex, then a full resource plan may be required. This plan would define what skills are needed, how many and when.

Clear responsibilities to achieve the sub-outcomes

3.10 Financial plan

What is the budget? What is the financial plan for the project? What are the projected costs going to be like?
How will the finances of the project be managed? This is the cost and the budget forecast profiles, they need to be defined at the start of the contract.

Budget profiles

The budget profile for the duration of the project should be detailed enough for each team to know and understand their budget. The actual cost can be allocated against the corresponding budget.

To enable the finances to be managed then budget profiles, cost forecast profiles and actual cost profiles, Fig 3.13 graphs with "s" curves, need to be produced and maintained updated to establish any variances every week or month.

Defined project budget and cost profiles

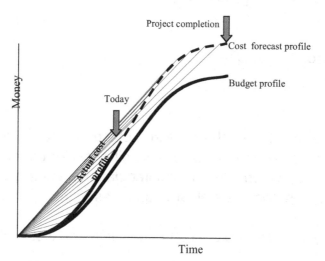

Fig 3.13 Budget, actual cost and cost forecast profiles

The graph shows a project overrunning time and cost. It is the role of the Project Manager to ensure actions are taken to recover any overruns and deliver the project targets.

Work breakdown structure (WBS)

For complex projects, the WBS should be developed from the logical plan, and the more detailed programme, and reflect the business structure and responsibilities, and reflect the cost coding structure, Fig 3.14.

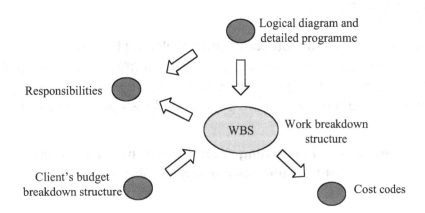

Fig 3.14 Connecting logical diagram to WBS, budget, cost, responsibilities

The client's own budget breakdown structure may influence the WBS.

In this way, the team leaders will know their tasks, from the programme, have a corresponding budget, and understand what they are spending. This means they are also managing a mini-business.

3.11 Risks

What are the risks of not achieving the project outcome?
How are these risks going to be managed to mitigate their effect on the project completion date?

The project risks are those that prevent the project outcome from being achieved on time and in full, and need to be linked to the logical diagram and hence the detailed programme.

Current difficulties

Often the approach to risk identification on projects does not link up to the delivery of the project.

Sometimes risks have been brainstormed at the start of the project with people who are fresh to it, and have not developed sufficient understanding of the project or its outcome. In this case, these people may have identified risks that they have encountered in their past, it reflects a fear within them rather than reflecting the project.

On a particular project a brainstorming event took place, a day after award, and over 200 risks were listed, many were not valid, and it took 18 months to re-categorise and reconsider the risks into something that was logical and meaningful. This was very time consuming and hence costly.

Linking risks to outcome

If the above steps of defining the outcome and developing the logical diagram are taken, then the risks are the non-achievement of the logical diagram and the project's outcome. This aligns the risk approach directly to the success of the project. These are the internal risks of the project, which are within the project leader's control and influence.

Defining and mitigating risks to the non-achievement of the outcome and logical diagram

---

There may be other external factors that also have to be considered as external risks and must also be identified.

Management of risk

The management of risk is different to risk management. Risk management is the traditional approach to managing programmes, and the likelihood and severity of risks associated with the carrying out of work.

There are numerous other risks that are often not considered as such, these are listed below, this is the management of risks. In order to achieve the best possible outcome, these risks have to be mitigated.

To manage risks effectively, the following have to be in place.

- o Having the right leader for the role, behaviour, role model and personality. This is the biggest risk of all. If the leader has the wrong personality, then he will struggle to get the project performing
- o In order to develop the right relationships with the client and key stakeholders, the personalities have to match. The project leader has to develop a clear understanding of stakeholders' needs and values (personal and corporate)
- o Having the right staff in the right role

- Having the right behaviour and personality of the top management that supports the team. The top management have to be role models. This behaviour will soon be reflected downwards within their teams
- Clear definition and analysis of the defined outcomes, direction (vision, mission) of the project
- Ensuring that there is the right values and culture, to achieve the best result
- Clear analysis of what would prevent the outcomes in the logical plan, obstacles, from happening
- Qualitative and quantitative risks analysis of the risks to achieving the outcomes, i.e. the traditional approach to risk management
- Clear definition and analysis defining the performance outcome of any technology to be implemented, this goes beyond the implementation of the technology or software
- Core problem analysis core reasons of why a crisis, or poor performance, has occurred.
- A logical programme of works that is resource linked e.g. critical chain project management
- Clear team outcome and purpose, with date and a plan for completion
- Effective communications by the top management, ensuring that all staff know their role and objectives, and how they fit into the direction of the project, soft and hard communication.
- Monitoring performance of the project and also the performance of the staff in the delivery of the outcomes

There are many techniques that help mitigate this list of risks, although many of these are not necessarily considered as risk management techniques.

Some typical risk management techniques include:

- Qualitative methods - likelihood and severity of risks
- Quantitative methods - numerical analysis of the probability of risks occurring
- Monte Carlo simulation - analyses various probability levels of each task on a project programme to determine the most likely overall probability for the project
- Decision tree analysis - identifies the probability of risks and costs of each available logical path within the decision tree
- Sensitivity analysis - helps to determine the uncertainty of elements of the project
- Cost risk analysis - this produces an "S-curve" of the probability of overrunning the cost estimate
- Strengths, weaknesses, opportunities, and threats (SWOT)
- Checklists
- Assumptions analysis

- o Diagramming techniques
- o System or process flow charts
- o Influence diagrams

Other techniques that help to mitigate risks are listed below, many of which are covered in this book:

- o 5PM
- o Strategic thinking, 4Qs
- o Logical diagrams, logic of necessity analysis
- o Cause-and-effect logical analysis
- o Analysis of the obstacles preventing objectives from being achieved
- o Minimising the impact of uncertainty on the project due date
- o Project's core problem analysis
- o Conflict analysis
- o Personality profiling
- o Critical chain project management
- o Needs analysis

This book is about mitigating project risk to develop the best possible outcome.

3.12 Supporting processes

The value stream, or the end to end process that adds value to the product, service and results that the client needs is normally the project programme.

The programme itself is a process, one of developing the project, product, service to deliver the required outcome for the client.

Are there any supporting processes of the project which support the achievement of the outcome or process model? These should be defined and include:

Company governance
- o Legal compliance
- o Industry compliance

- o Health and Safety
- o Environmental
- o HR
- o Financial
- o Procurement

Project governance
- o Interface processes
- o Change control
- o Client Approvals
- o Client handovers, commissioning and testing

These processes should have a clear outcome, and purpose, person responsible for achieving that outcome/purpose and thereby be managed as a mini-project.

Where appropriate the process outcome must be aligned to the sub-outcomes on the logical diagram or programme.

3.13 Culture

Crucially, what is the required culture of the project? What are the values? It is the values which define the culture and determine the degree of project success.

The culture is normally a reflection of the leadership.

What are the behaviours and the role models required by the senior managers for the project to be successful? A team will adopt the behaviour and attitude of the project leader. So it is essential for the project leader to have the right behaviour.

Defined values, behaviours, role models to create the required culture for success

---

Effective project management comes from having the right culture, this is made up of the values, attitude and behaviour, Fig 3.15.

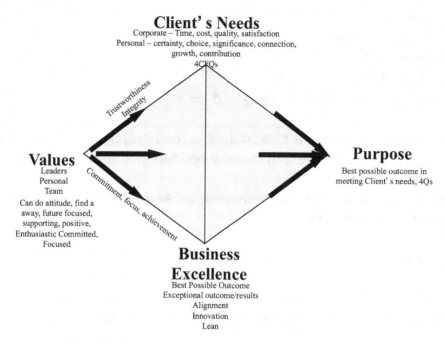

Fig 3.15 Foundation for all successful projects

If the team are really passionate about what they are doing, and if they understand their compelling purpose, and if they understand their clients corporate and emotional needs and values, and they deliver the best possible outcome in achieving those needs whilst always focusing on their purpose, then they will achieve success in the eyes of the client.

This is the foundation of all successful projects and businesses.

3.14   Senior Management commitment

There may be senior managers who are not directly part of the project, but can influence the project's outcome. So what do the senior managers have to do to demonstrate their commitment?

The commitment of senior management to the project should be an active and visible involvement in the project. If senior management are interested in their staff's work then motivation their staff increases. It is so important to have someone senior who is seen to be fully supportive of the project. This gives the right messages.

However, too often influential managers do not see this as important, and then they wonder why the best result is not achieved.

Ensuring senior management commitment and support

3.15 Communication

The word "communication" or "comm-uni-cation" is the "common union of action". This is the communication of the common direction that all the team need to understand and be aligned to.

How is the project strategy and performance going to be communicated to the project staff?
How is staff feedback going to be managed to make improvements?

Effective communication of strategy and performance to everyone

---

The project strategy document, when completed and approved, must be communicated to the:
  o Project sponsor, client
  o Project team members
  o Other persons who are or may be involved or affected by the project
  o Supply chain

Also the progress of the project must be regularly communicated to all those who need to know. For complex projects a detailed communication plan may be needed outlining the modes of communication, with the communication purpose, for
  o External stakeholders
  o Internal stakeholders

3.16 Project definition

If the project is going to be really successful, each one of the following topics needs to be planned by the project leader, at the start of the project.

Strategic planning

The project strategy needs to cover the following topics.

  o Context
  o Outcome/vision/destination Q1
  o Purpose/mission/aim/direction Q2
  o Problem to overcome or opportunity Q3
  o Logical diagram, overall timescale Q4
  o Client's needs, values, success definition 4CFQs
  o Scope, deliverables

- o Resources plan, number and skilled resources, responsibilities, and reporting lines, organisational chart
- o Detained programme
- o Financial plan - budget profile, cost forecast, actual cost
- o Measures - aligned to outcome
- o Supporting processes - change control, approvals, interfaces
- o Communication plan, of strategy and progress
- o Key risks
- o Procurement strategy
- o Culture, values
- o Senior Management commitment

This list may have to vary depending on the size and nature of the project.

Managing the Project

How is the project going to be monitored, reviewed and reported?
How will continuous improvement be carried out? Who is responsible for continuous improvement? How will problems be highlighted and overcome?

These processes for measuring, monitoring, reviewing, reporting, problem solving, and continuous improvement need to be clearly identified within that strategy.

Key meetings will need to be identified with clear
- o Purpose of the meeting
- o Outcome of the meeting
- o Agenda
- o attendees

Project Strategy Document

When a leader is in place, one of the first things he has to do is produce this project strategy, for both the strategic planning and management of the project.

If possible, some of the team members need to be involved with the formulation of parts of this strategy. By doing so they are more involved and thereby more motivated.

Clear project strategy is defined

When the above has been clearly defined it should be written up as the project strategy document, or a number of documents for a complex project, agreed and signed off by the project sponsor.

Start Up

This strategy document is then used to brief the team, at the project start up meeting. They should have a clear understanding of their own responsibilities, what the big picture is of the project is, what the project is there to achieve, who the stakeholders are, what their particular part in the project is, and what the culture is.

The project strategy document is a communication tool, as well as a project definition tool.

**Start up meeting to communicate strategy, and
ensure every one understand their role**

By doing this at the start of the project, the project team should have clarity of the project, and be committed to the project, particularly if they have been involved with the formulation of the project strategy. Their role will need to be aligned so that their own outcomes fit within this project strategy framework.

This will provide the best opportunity to start the project with sufficient clarity.

Chapter 3—The Best Project Strategy

What have you discovered about project management?

How can you apply this to your projects?

What ideas has it given you to improve your project management?

What are some actions you can take to start managing your projects to achieve the best possible outcome?

1.

2.

3.

4.

5.

The Best from the Project Staff

4 The Best from the Project Staff

It is essential for the project leader to motivate his staff to deliver their best, since it is the people that will make the project successful.

If the project had the best systems and processes, but no people, then the project could not achieve anything. Conversely, if the project had the right people who were really motivated, enthusiastically, committed and dedicated but with no or poor systems and processes, then they would make things work and achieve probably 80% of the potential, if not more.

Right people, motivated, enthusiastic, committed

It is the people that really count in project management. If you can get the best out of your people then you are likely to achieve the potential for the project.

The project staff have their own personal needs, and if the project leader is going to get the best out of the project team, then those needs have to be satisfied.

This section is about how to motivate people.

4.1 Belief in the Project Leader

To get the best out of your people they have to believe in the project leader, his experience, knowledge, skills and abilities.

Since people believe in the person first before what he says, then the project leader's behaviour has to be right. As a project leader walks around his project office, his staff see him and his behaviour. They will interpret his:
- Physiology - his body language has to be positive, forward, confident, determined
- Focus - he focuses on the future, forward, can do attitude, determined
- Language - his language that he uses has to have energy, enthusiasm, determination with the right tone
- Image - he needs to look the part, professional

People will reflect the behaviour of the project leader. If he is not positive, enthusiastic then staff will reflect this, and the project will suffer.

So the project leader's behaviour will help generate the staff belief in him.

4.2   Belief in the project

The project staff have to believe in the project, believe that the project is viable, believe that the outcome can be achieved and is worthwhile.

The project staff need to understand:
- o   What is the outcome of the project? Q1
- o   Why must this outcome has to be achieved, and by what date? Q2
- o   What is the problem that the project must solve? Q3
- o   What has to be in place to achieve the outcome? Q4
- o   What are the client's needs and values? 4CFQS
- o   What is the scope and deliverables of the project?
- o   What is success? How is this defined? Who defines it?
- o   How is success of the project going to be measured?
- o   What are the benefits to the business?
- o   Who are the project sponsor, the project manager, the team?
- o   What are their roles and responsibilities and their role and outcome?
- o   What is the realistic timescale to achieve the outcome?
- o   What are the risks to the non-delivery of the outcome?
- o   How are we to monitor, review, report and improve to ensure the outcome is achieved?
- o   What commitment do we need from Senior Managers/Directors?

If possible the project staff need to be involved with defining/understanding the above to get them. The more involved the staff are then the more they "buy-into" it.

Purpose = Motivation

The communication of the project strategy or plan is therefore critical to getting the project team on board and committed.

Staffs' belief in the project leader's ability and the project

---

4.3   Benefit to them

The project staff also have to believe what they will gain from the success of the project, for example that they will:

- o   Be recognised for the effort that they put in
- o   Be promoted
- o   Stay in a position that they like

- o   Get a pay rise, or bonus
- o   Other benefits to them

If there is no benefit to them then this will reduce motivation. Too often people are not recognised for the effort that put in and their morale is effected.

Once the staff have this belief in the project leader, belief the project and believe in the benefits the project will bring to them, then in order to ensure they are motivated throughout the life of the project, their emotional needs will have to be fully satisfied.

4.4   Emotional needs

The motivation of the project staff can be summed up as satisfying their six emotional needs, as defined by Robbins A. (2001) who is a world leader in personal development.

Project team's needs aligned to those of his client and Board

---

The role of the project leader is to motivate their staff. To do this they have to align and satisfy the needs of his staff, and the supply chain, to those of the client and Board.

Project team Possible examples of the six emotional human needs	
Certainty	1. the team member understands the project, the project outcomes, the purpose, stakeholder's needs, the risks, plan of action 2. they have to be certain of their role, and what is expected of them 3. they must be certain about their ability to achieve that role
Choice	1. some people like to be able to choose how to perform their role rather than being dictated to, they like to be stretched, they like variety 2. some people like to be told exactly what to do and how to do it, so the right balance has to be achieved
Significance	1. they like to feel significant, they are important 2. their role is important 3. they are listened to, their views are heard 4. their work is valued
Connection, Rapport	1. they feel that they are part of the team, feeling of teamwork 2. they feel a close connection and a close rapport with the project leader 3. they feel that they can give and receive positive feedback

Growth	1. they feel they are learning 2. they feel they are developing and understanding more 3. they are growing through mentoring, coaching
Contribution	1. they feel they are contributing to their own success 2. they feel they are contributing to the success of the team and project 3. they feel they are contributing to the success of the business

Fig 4.1 Project staff's emotional needs

These are examples of the key emotional needs that motivate people, Fig 4.1. The main one is certainty. Certainty that we know where we are going and what we are doing. This is the primary emotional need of us all.

The project leader will have to produce their own list that suits their project staff. To do this the project leader will have to get to know their staff, to listen to them and understand their aspirations and views.

Project team's needs are met, and are motivated

4.5   Valuable and Valued

If all these emotional needs are being satisfied and each of the project team is really positive about:

- o   feeling valuable (have the skills and ability to perform)
- o   feeling valued (are recognised by their team, boss and business)

then they will be truly motivated and provide the extra effort, or passion, to succeed. If all the project team feel this way, then the full potential of the project can be achieved.

The more the project team feel valuable and valued, the more they will give

However, if only one emotional need is not being satisfied, that person will not be motivated to their full potential and will not be giving their best.

It is up to the project leader, or the leader of any team, to ensure that their team's needs are satisfied if he wants to get the best out of them.

These emotional needs can be applied to any business relationship, and any home or social relationship.

In order to develop the team, the project leader must be, himself, trustworthy. And trust his team. He must do what he says he will do, this will create trust within the team. This trust, with the project staff's belief in both the project leader and the project, and their own needs being met, will create empowerment and commitment.

The more the leader is involved and patient with their staff, the more committed they become

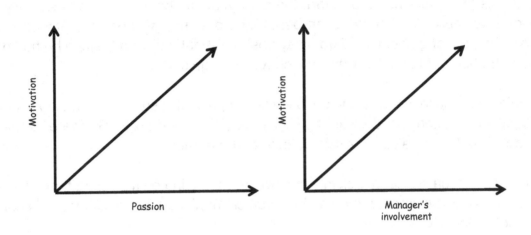

Fig 4.2 Motivation increases with passion, and also manager's involvement

The more someone is passionate about their role then the more they will be motivated, Fig 4.2. Also the more their manager is involved with their staff and review their work, in a positive way, then the more motivated the staff would become. Their emotional needs would be satisfied.

Motivation example—Engineering Manager

An engineering manager once received a report from a recently recruited engineer who was part of his team. He wanted the report to be the best, so without saying anything he immediately flipped through the report, confronted the author and highlighted the things that were not right with it. He said "Oh, you haven't done this, you haven't done that, you haven't done the other", pointing to the particular sections.

The engineering manager was doing this with the best of intentions, but he was criticising the report and its author. This immediately lowered the author's feeling of significance. By doing this, the engineering manager was effectively raising his own level of significance above that of the author's, i.e. the engineering manager was saying "I am better than you are—I know more than you know".

The new engineer went away feeling dispirited, and disgruntled. Would he be willing to update the report the way the engineering manager wanted it without delay? No. There would be some sort of grudge, there would be a delay, there would be a reluctance to provide the updates. The author may even be fearful of presenting anything again to the engineering manager in fear of being criticised.

On the other hand, if the engineering manager had identified all of the good things and effort that the engineer had done within the report—and there were bound to be lots of good things (e.g. the amount of effort, the presentation style) and then to actually say "how can we make this section even better, and also this section, and also this next section" then the engineer would go away positive about the report, since he had done his best, he had put in a lot of effort which was recognised.

He would be willing to go away and update it and improve it in such a way the engineering manager had wanted it and would be more likely to do it quickly. So the engineering manager would have raised the significance of the author.

This is giving "negative" feedback in a positive way focusing on the future that motivates the author to achieve improvements. Just a quick thank you for the effort put in can be really motivating.

The past cannot be corrected/changed, the report had been drafted, so the engineering manager should only look to the future "what else can we do to make it even better". Moving from a past focused to a future focused approach will increase motivation.

4.6   Aligning people

To motivate people in any business, if they know what they really want to do, and if these are what the business wants them to do, and they are given the support, help, training to achieve them, then they will be motivated.

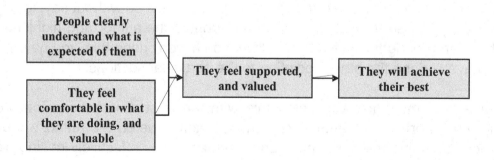

Fig 4.3 Aligning and supporting people

**Project team are aligned, understand what is required from
them, feel supported and hence give their best**

The Supply Chain's needs

To achieve the best for the project, it is important to get the best out of the supply chain.

For the supply chain to say that the project is, or will be, successful then the project leader has to manage the supply chain's expectations and their personal six emotional needs.

These particular needs could be information, access, or a whole list of things that the project leader and his team have to satisfy to get the supply chain to perform their best.

In the past, there have been relationships that have been based on hiding behind the contract, and not working together, contractual tension and claims have therefore resulted, stage 1, Fig 2.2. This creates inefficiencies, underperformance, unnecessary cost, friction, lost profits and claims. All parties involved suffer except the lawyers.

If we can try and overcome this and satisfy the needs of the parties right from the start, and develop those relationships, then the chances of getting the best out of the supply chain are far higher. The benefits would be a sustainable long-term relationship which could include:

- o Continuity of work
- o Sustainable profit
- o Enhanced reputation

Some examples of the specific needs of the key supply chain are included in the following table.

Key Supply Chain Possible examples of the 6 emotional needs	
Certainty	1. that they will get required details of scope of work, specification, drawings, orders, quantities, in a timely manner to perform the work most effectively 2. that they will have the required access and support to be able to perform
Choice	1. that they are allowed to decide on the best way of how they will perform their work 2. they can choose what they need and when they need in order to perform

Significance	1. that their views will be heard of how best to perform their role 2. their expertise is recognised
Connection, Rapport	1. that they are able to work together, with the project team, to resolve issues for mutual benefit, 2. that they have a good relationship
Growth	1. that they can learn, gain knowledge to help grow their business and the project
Contribution	1. that they contributes to the their business' success, profit, market share and reputation 2. that they contribute to the project's success

Fig 4.4 Supply chain emotional needs

Supply chain's needs are met, then they will perform

The supply chain must be treated as members of the project staff in order to get the best out of them.

Chapter 4—The Best from your Project Staff

What have you discovered about project management?

How can you apply this to your projects?

What ideas has it given you to improve your project management?

What are some actions you can take to start managing your projects to achieve the best possible outcome?

1.

2.

3.

4.

5.

The Best Project Performance

5   The Best Project Performance

5.1   Uncertainty

As every project is unique then there is always uncertainty, this is a fact of life for projects and project management. Invariably this uncertainty causes overruns.

There is a widely quoted figure that 80% of all projects worldwide overrun on time or cost. So the art of project management is to minimise the effects of uncertainty on the project completion date.

**80 % of projects worldwide overrun time or cost,
therefore existing practices are insufficient**

Morris & Hough, 1987, have listed some of the factors that affect project overruns:
- o Poor project definition, complexity, underestimated difficulty and cost, quantities and scope increases, underestimating costs, support costs.
- o High risk, poor risk management
- o Engineering and design changes, design faults, technological advance, uncertainty, unforeseen technical difficulties
- o Payment difficulties, funding availability, cash flow, inflation, interest charges
- o Scheduling changes
- o Increased safety requirements
- o Shortage of materials
- o Contractor's financial problems
- o Late approvals, late information
- o Insufficient training, Incompetence
- o Poor industrial relations management, strikes, labour shortage problems
- o Adverse or unforeseen site conditions
- o Impact on, and by, the local community

Is there a method that would minimise the effects of uncertainty from affecting the project completion date? If so what it is?

This section discusses a technique, *critical chain project management*, that minimises the effects of uncertainty on the delivery date.

5.2   Critical Chain Project management

In this section, we will be exploring a solution that will:

- o manage the effects of those uncertainties, that are under the project leader's control, on the project's due date
- o minimise the effects of those uncertainties that are beyond the control of the project manager.

This gives the **Best Project Performance,** and removes, or minimises the uncertainty affecting the project's completion date, excluding any unforeseen major external factor.

The best project performance

Dr. Eli Goldratt related his "Theory of Constraints" (TOC) approach to project management in his book *Critical Chain* (1997). It is a novel developing the concepts of critical chain techniques that will be discussed in more detail in this section.

This section is based on this Critical Chain philosophy and experiences gained in the last 20 years implementing critical chain on real projects.

Newbold (1998), in his application of TOC and critical chain to project management argues that ". . . all the solutions [to the problems that we have discussed earlier] . . . have been around for at least 20 years. However, since the problems still exist, the solutions must be inadequate."

The solution to these individual problems are what we will call localised solutions, which only affect one element of the project overall and can damage the project elsewhere.

What the critical chain philosophy provides is not a solution to all of the problems identified, but an holistic mechanism that minimises the effects of these difficulties on the completion date.

Since the goal of the project is likely to be to complete the project on time and in full, then the solution developed must provide the best project performance in achieving this goal.

5.3   Common project difficulties

Some common difficulties in project management that critical chain identifies, from Newbold (1998), Baylis (2001), Goldratt (1997) include:

Estimating tasks

It is impossible to estimate something exactly, unless it is in a highly repetitive environment such as in a factory.

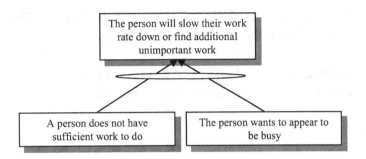

Fig 5.1Cause and effect diagram of work filling the allotted time

Projects are normally a development of something unique which takes time to achieve. Hence the estimates of task durations are only an estimate, and are the judgement of the estimator at the time, based on experiences and knowledge.

If the estimator had a good similar experience, everything went well, then the task duration may be underestimated.

Conversely, if the estimator has had a bad experience, everything went wrong, he may overestimate the task duration.

In either case the estimates cannot reflect what may happen as it hasn't happened yet, it is difficult to predict the future.

Multitasking

Multi-tasking is when people often switch between several tasks before completing any of them, often as demanded by their manager. Newbold (1998) therefore argues that ". . . . all tasks will take much longer to complete than they need to".

This means that there are no clear defined priorities for carrying out these tasks, or the order that they should be completed in. People often carry out "urgent" tasks, demanded by their manager, rather than the "important" ones to complete the project on time.

Multi-tasking is one of the most damaging aspects to the delivery of projects on time.

Measures

Newbold (1998) says that ". . . arbitrary measurements can sap intensity and drain productivity."

Since people behave as they are measured, because they want an easy time and do not want to be criticised, they will take action to achieve that measure.

However, often the measures do not point the person in the right direction to deliver the business outcomes and, if this is the case, then the effort is wasted.

Parkinson's Law

People can stay busy by ". . . causing work to expand to fill the available capacity. This is a major cause of lost productivity" Newbold (1998).

If people are given a target date then they will adjust their work rate to suit that date. So any early finishes will not be gained.

People will expand their work to fit the time available.

Student syndrome

Some people may start an important task to a deadline, such as producing a report, but, believing there is spare time, they stop working and move to other activities. The deadline looms and time becomes very tight, they then start to work in earnest but then something happens which delays them and they struggle to complete the task on time.

Spare time on an important task is often wasted at the start of that task.

Example
Students from a university were given a research project to complete within 2 weeks. There was approximately 1 week's worth of effort, but they still asked for an extension of time of 1 week. On this occasion the Professor granted them the extension of time making a total of 3 weeks to do 1 week's worth of effort.

However, since students enjoy being students and the party life, they used all their spare time (2 weeks) enjoying themselves and only started work at the beginning of the last week. But half way through the week there was a 21st birthday party, which they all 'had" to go to. It lasted all night and the following day they had to sleep it off. So they lost a day on their 5 day programme, 20%.

Now time is very short, they had to work late into the night to complete the project, becoming stressed, cutting corners, and quality suffered just to get it in. They were so late they asked for another ½ day extension of time.

This is called student syndrome and applies throughout the majority of projects and businesses.

Setting up time

". . . When there is multitasking, people are frequently switching between tasks, because they must show regular progress on each task. The time needed to switch between tasks is called "setting up" Newbold (1998). This is hidden extra cost since this setting up takes to re-adjust to.

Using more people to do a task

Newbold (1998) argues that ". . . there quickly comes a point where adding more people actually increases the time it takes to do a job, through increased communication requirements"

This is because any new persons drafted in is likely to cause elements of chaos until they become adjusted to their role. They have to take up time of the existing people to learn their role, there may be resentment with people being drafted in, a loss of morale and confidence, and greater communication is required with a larger number of people now involved.

There is no hurry

Often there is an attitude that the work will be finished when it is finished. There is no hurry. This is certainly so for a number of different cultures across the world, it can be a national attitude.

Starting or finishing early

". . . The penalty for being late is much greater than the reward for being early" argues Newbold (1998) but this is often not appreciated since rewards are not often clearly identified in contracts.

So there is often no incentive to finish early. If they did finish and hand over the task early, they may put extra pressure on themselves for next time and as most people want an easy life, then they are unlikely to hand over the task early.

There may be "urgent" demands for them to do something else, and so they may not start on time.

Murphy's Law

"If something can go wrong, then it will go wrong". This is called Murphy's Law. The task in question will take far longer than the original estimated time.

There is a lot of uncertainty within a project as the diagram illustrates, Fig 5.2. How do we overcome this uncertainty?

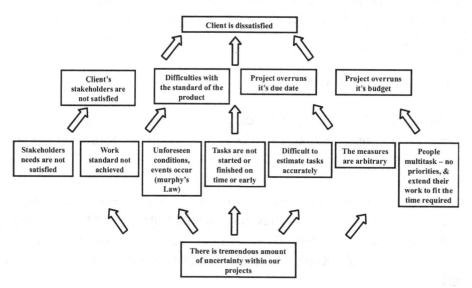

Fig 5.2 Key uncertainty causing dissatisfaction

It is impossible to eliminate this uncertainty. So what we need is a solution that can overcome the effects of uncertainty and provide us with certainty of completing the project on time, in full, to the client's needs.

Minimising the effects of uncertainty on the project due date

---

This needs an approach that protects us from the effects of uncertainty to enable us to:-
   o deliver the project on time or ahead of time
   o carry out more projects in a multi-project environment
   o deliver the project within budget
   o satisfy the client in terms of standard, time and budget
   o meets the client's needs and values

The solution must focus on the overall delivery of the project, rather than the individual solution to individual isolated problems. There must be an holistic solution rather than a local optima solution.

5.4   Effects of human behaviour

In order to understand the effects of uncertainty on a project, we have to understand the effects of human behaviour on tasks, and how those behaviours affect the due date completion.

Behaviours in Estimating Task Duration

If we are asked to estimate the duration of a task, do we ever know:-
   o   the exact minimum time we'll need? Can the task be more quickly?
   o   the exact average time of the task?
   o   the exact actual time the task will take?

The duration of every task is a statistical quantity and therefore has probability fluctuations.

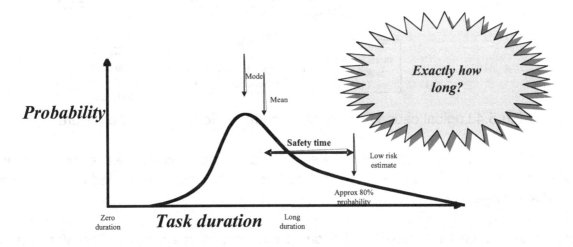

Fig 5.3 Probability curve of task duration

Can we expect interruptions as we perform our work? Have there been problems in the past that have caused the task to overrun?

So what might happen, to us personally, if we used unrealistically short estimates of duration and the task overruns, how would our boss respond? Then the next time we quote for a similar task he will insist on the shorter time. This creates stress, pressure and increases the risk of overrunning. This increases the risk of being criticised. So we don't report an early finish.

As normally we do not like to be criticised, we tend to quote a low-risk estimate (e.g. 80-90% probability of achieving) that is low personal risk.

We all want an easy life, with no criticism, and so we tend to quote task durations that we could easily achieve e.g. 80-90% probability. So task durations tend to have "safety time" automatically built in.

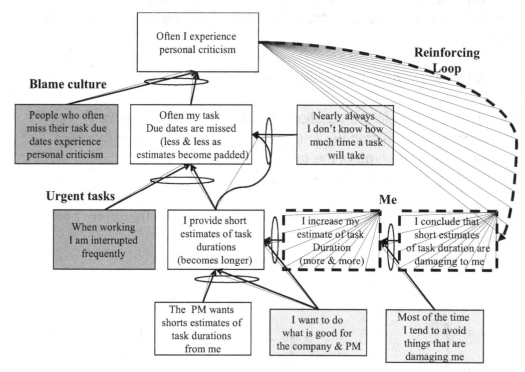

Fig 5.4 Logical cause and effect diagram reinforcing a blame culture

However, each time that we experience personal criticism when we overrun the time duration, we go through the reinforcing loop and the durations estimated the next time round are longer.

This continues until the schedule becomes too long for management comfort. Then they cut the durations, but by doing so they lose the buy-in from us since we did not agree to the cut, and we can identify all sorts of reasons why the cut duration will not be achieved since we want to save ourselves from further criticism.

The severity of this game will depend on the blame culture that has been generated by the behaviour of the top management. The more aggressive they are the more unlikely they will receive realistic task quotations.

5.5   Effects of these behaviours on projects

So what is the effect of this on a project?

Project performance

The following diagram represents a simple three-task project.

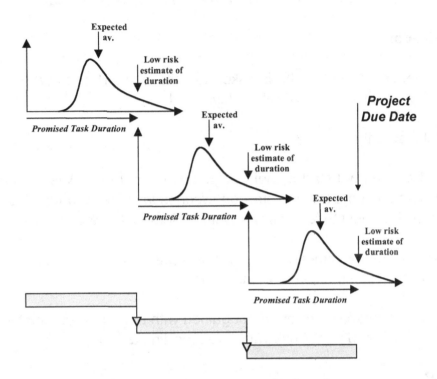

Fig 5.5 Simple project with 3 tasks

So if we take these behaviours whereby each task has safety time built into it and we do not report and early finish, then what is the likelihood of the project being finished early, within budget? Very low. These types of behaviours will cause the project to overrun. It relates to the culture and behaviour/attitude of management.

This is likely to the main cause of the 80% of project overruns.

Targets

What are the effects of setting targets on the project performance. Targets are dates, milestones, for both time and budgets that have to be achieved.

Human nature will tend to use up any spare time at the start of the task duration, Student's Syndrome. We normally expand the work to fit the time available, Parkinson's Law. The target becomes the focus. But, as any spare time is normally used up early, and something unexpected happens, Murphy's Law, the completion of the task to time is at risk. So tasks tend not to be completed early, they overrun time or cost/budget.

Is the project very likely to see the effect of an early finish? No.

Do we aim to meet the date rather than finish early? Yes.

So milestone dates, and targets, do not create the desired behaviour.

Example—Report

On Monday morning at 9am, John is asked to write a report and hand it in by Friday evening, but John knows that it is only 3 days' work.

When will John start the report?

It is unlikely that John will start straight away and hand it in on Wednesday evening, 2 days early. John is more likely to start on Wednesday aiming to take the full allotted time and submitting it just before the due date of 5pm on Friday.

But what if something else happens? John is under pressure and risks either overrunning the end date or submitting a sub-standard report.

So savings in the timescale are often not gained with the report completed early, and hence there is increased risk of overruns. No reporting an early finish.

Example—Petrol

If we fill our car up with petrol/diesel, and our target is to fill up with £50, how much petrol will we end up putting in the car?

How often will we end up with £49.99? Never.
How often will we put in exactly £50.00? Sometimes.
How often will we just exceed the target and put in £50.01? Most of the time.

So if we have a target to achieve, human nature will aim for the target and often just go over it, so we overrun.

Urgent Tasks and Important tasks

Imagine that we are working on an important task, it has a due date and time is short.

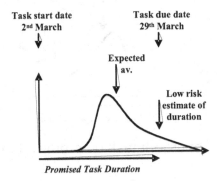

Fig 5.6 Promised task duration

Does it happen that some other task becomes more "urgent" than the currently scheduled promised task?

Are we often asked to do something "now" by our manager? The manger feels important and so dictates that we do a task now. We have to do what we are told to do as we want to get promotion.

But what happens to the important task? It gets delayed and there is an increased risk of overrunning the due date. If there is continual delay to the start of the important task, an overrun will be certain.

Some people like the adrenaline rush that they get from working at the very last minute. They do not plan and rush from one urgent task to another, there is no prioritisation of tasks.

Does this occur in your business or, on your project? Do you or your business spend much of its time fire fighting?

Often fires are "created" by the business so that they can put them out and get praise.

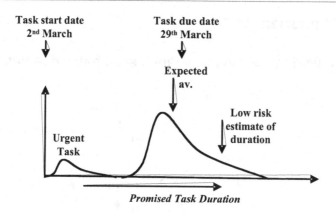

Fig 5.7 Effect of urgent task on promised task duration

5.6   Effects on the project performance

What is the effect on our projects?

- o Our projects are often late - time overrun
- o We often overrun our budgets - cost overrun
- o We often don't deliver all the features that we promised - specifications or standards are cut
- o We often work overtime - extra cost, lower morale
- o Everything in the schedule looks critical - fire fighting
- o We seem to reschedule constantly - lack of focus

But where is the real damage? Is it just to the current project, or is it wider effecting market share?

The real damage could be that competitors may enter into our niche market and drive the market price and profits downwards.

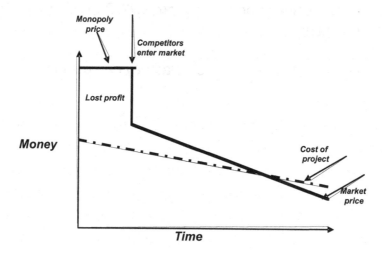

Fig 5.8 The true loss is in the lost market share

To avoid competitors entering the market, we should use the latest techniques to minimise cost, increase market share and maximise our profits to keep us ahead of the competition.

So what is the core issue of project management?
Is there a single core issue of project management that controls all these behaviours?

During any project there are numerous changes, and it is difficult to stop these changes, or uncertainties, from occurring.
However, since the goal of the project is to deliver the project on time (to the due date), within budget and to specification, the single core issue of a project is not that there is uncertainty during the project's life, but, how that uncertainty is managed to minimise the effect on the project's due date.

This is the management of project's core issue, and will be explained below.

5.7 Holistic solution

So the solution must be a global or holistic solution for the complete system that makes up the project and all the businesses or supplier/sub-contractors that contribute to that system. This solution is a project management philosophy called "Critical Chain" as developed by Eli Goldratt and described in his novel of the same name.

Developing a holistic solution for the complete system

Newbold (1998) stated that ". . . we need a better approach to dealing with uncertainty". He goes on to say that:-
"We have an approach to scheduling and logistics that protect us from the effects of uncertainty. People are focused on global (system-wide) improvements rather than local ones. Everyone understands and accepts the policies, procedures and measurements that apply to them. We believe we can make dramatic improvements"

It is the holistic solution of how we manage the effects of uncertainty on the completion date of the project that is described in the next section.

Within the project business, to ensure the best project performance by applying the critical chain philosophy, we need to understand:

- o   what to change
- o   what to change to
- o   how to implement the change

But first of all we will consider a traditional single project.

5.8   Traditional single project

A traditional project programme has been produced in Fig 5.9.

The tasks are arranged in logical finish to start sequence as indicated by the arrows. Each task is identified by a task number and duration in days eg "1.20" is task 1. 20 days duration.

This is a typical programme, Fig 5.9, which includes safety time within each task. This programme, with associated cost plan, has been agreed for the project.

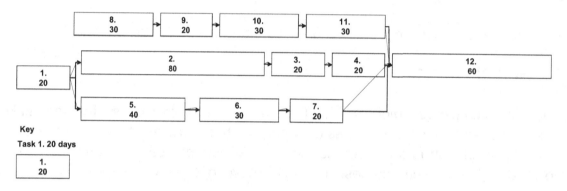

Fig 5.9 Traditional project programme

Traditionally there is "float" or spare time built into each task to cope with any uncertainty within that task. This "float" is managed by the person carrying out the task and it is this approach to managing any spare time, by people carrying out the task, this is the project's core problem.

What is the critical Path?

The critical path is the longest sequence of dependent events. In this case, the critical path goes through tasks 1, 2, 3, 4, 12, and totals 200 days. The critical path is task driven.

With this logical programme, each task has been estimated with a high level of probability (say 80%) of achieving the task duration.

It is like an extended spring, highly variable with time.

But what are the difficulties associated with this programme?

Can this project be delivered to time and cost as currently programmed?

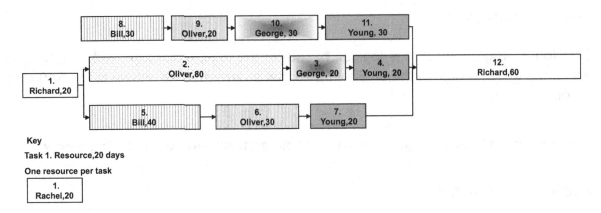

Fig 5.10 Traditional programme but with resources assigned

The different shading and names represent the different resources. We are assuming that the resources are unique to the project, that they are hard to find and hire quickly. For example, this could reflect a design office which has a defined set of resources and often it is difficult to employ new staff quickly.

As soon as the resources are assigned we can see overlaps with these resources: tasks 2,6,9, overlap; tasks 5,8 overlap; tasks 3,10 overlap; tasks 4,7,11 overlap.

So can this project be delivered to time and cost as currently programmed? No!

This programme has to be either extended by 60 days, or extra resources have to be found for the overlapping tasks. The realistic programme time is therefore 260 days and not the original 200 days. So immediately the original programme is flawed by time and cost.

We have already discussed the impact of human behaviour on tasks, and the likely effect of using up the "float" that exists within each of them. So any spare time built into the programme is allowed to be used by the task owners. Also that there is no reporting of an early finish.

There is a very high chance of the project overrunning.

So how can we overcome this? The next section explains the principles of critical chain project management.

5.9   Critical Chain Project Management (CCPM)

CCPM is normally used as an internal operational tool.

The key steps in producing a critical chain programme are described below

Traditional programme

Develop a programme that is logical, based on the logical diagram, with safety time within the tasks, similar to the original traditional programme as shown in Fig 5.10 with resources identified.

Develop a logical programme with estimated task duration including safety

---

Reduced programme

The purpose of the critical chain programme is to track the programme slippage and implement contingency plans if the slippage is too fast and too early. So the estimated duration is, at best, a good guess. There is no need to spend too much time to get a detailed analysis of the task duration.

To produce a critical chain project programme, all safety is taken out of each task. It does not matter how accurate this is.

Remove safety time from all tasks in programme

One can ask the question of the persons carrying out each task:
"If all went well, what is the best, or minimum time, that you could complete this task in?"
So the duration will be without any safety time, there is likely to be a 50 % probability of achieving this task duration and hence the project.

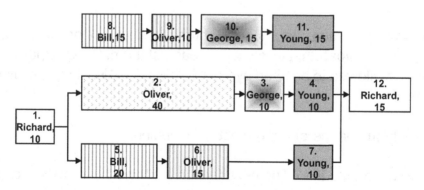

Fig 5.11 Programme without any safety time

Fig 5.11 represents the programme with all safety time removed. This is like a compressed spring, but the original project due date has not changed. In this case, each task has been reduced by 50%.

The 50% reduction has been used for illustration purposes, and has been used effectively on many projects. However, you can decide how much you to reduce the tasks, they can be reduced individually depending on the nature of the task. Normally in practice I use 30% reduction.

The project programme is now very vulnerable to uncertainties and if they occur, the due date would be threatened. So how do we protect the project completion date?

Resource conflict

Any resource conflict has to be removed. Fig 5.12 shows the programme with tasks 5,8 and 2,6,9 and 3,10 and 4,7,11 not conflicting, as indicated by the arrows.

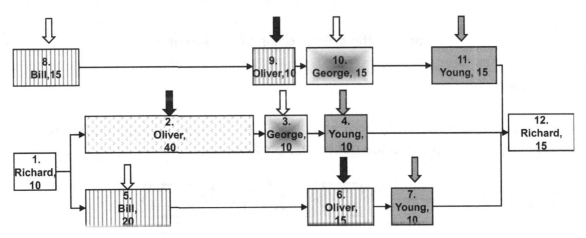

Fig 5.12 Remove any resource conflict

Remove resource conflict from programme

Critical Chain

The Critical Chain goes through the most overworked resource as well as through the task dependency starting at the first task and ending with the last task. It is this sequence of dependencies, both task and resource, that prevents the project from being completed in a shorter interval, given finite resources. The critical chain takes into account the resources as well as the tasks.

The most overworked resource is Oliver. So the critical chain must go through tasks 2,9,6 bust also starts at the beginning and end at the end.

So in this case, the critical chain goes through tasks 1,2,9,6,7,11,12 as shown with the highlighted boxes in Fig 5.13.

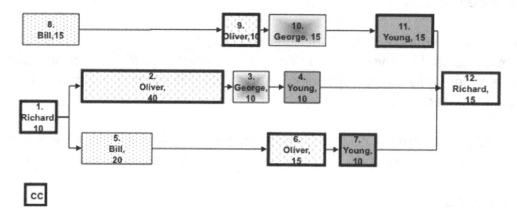

Fig 5.13 Critical chain is identified in bold

This is a completely different sequence than the critical path one identified earlier.

Identify the critical chain in programme

Protection

With the safety time removed, from each task, we have spare time that we can insert at strategic places to provide the necessary protection.

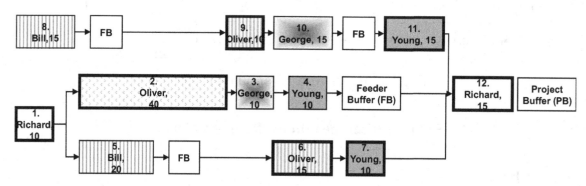

Fig 5.14 Strategically placing project and feeder buffers

Add the project and feeder buffers

There are 2 type of protection as indicated in Fig 5.14.

i) Project completion buffer (PB)

The project completion buffer protects the project completion date from uncertainties, slippages, that occur along the critical chain.

With all projects there should only be one project buffer which is placed at the end of the critical chain and just before the project's completion date.

The rule of thumb for the size of project buffer is that, the amount of time allowed should be around 1/3 of the total critical chain time.

In this case, the critical chain, tasks 1,2,9,6,7,11,12, which is 115 days, so the project buffer is 38 days.

However, if there is a high risk task which would have severe consequences if it went wrong, the size of the project completion buffer should be adjusted to suit the risk. So the size of the project buffer can be modified to suit the risk of potential overrun if that task goes wrong.

ii) Feeder buffers (FB)

The feeder lines are those lines that are parallel to the critical chain, and they feed into the critical chain. These are all the lines that are not in bold, Fig 5.14

The feeder buffers are located at the end of the feeder lines and immediately before they intersect with the critical chain. They protect the critical chain from any slippages along these feeder lines.

Feeder buffers are located just before the feeder lines leads into the critical chain, Fig 5.14 shows 4 feeder buffers
- FB after task 8 and just before CC task 9.
  Duration of 5 days which is 1/3 of the feeder line of 15days.
- FB after task 5 and just before CC task 6.
  Duration of 7 days which is 1/3 of the feeder line of 20days.
- FB after task 10 and just before CC task 11.
  Duration of 5 days which is 1/3 of the feeder line of 15days.
- FB after task 4 and just before CC task 12.
  Duration of 7 days which is 1/3 of the feeder line of 20days.

Again the size of the feeder buffers should be around 1/3 of the total time of the feeder line.

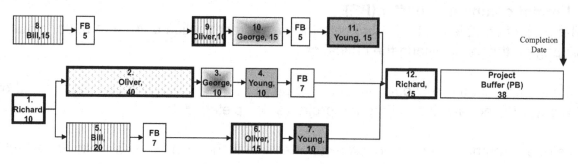

Fig 5.15 Completed critical chain plan

On any single project there should only be one project buffer but a number of feeder buffers.

Resource warnings

The buffers are now in place. The critical resources or people are those needed to work on a critical chain task. These are Richard, Oliver, Young, and Richard again following the CC tasks.

These resources must be kept up-to-date with when they are required to start. They need to be fully prepared so, when they are required to do so, they must stop all other work and concentrate on the critical task until it is completed, and handed over to the next resource.

These critical resources need to work at full steam on their critical tasks, and not on any other task, until it is completed. No multi-tasking.

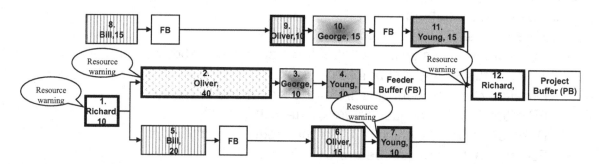

Fig 5.16 Warning critical resources to be prepared to start

Completion date

We now have constructed a critical chain programme and the completion date has been determined. However, if this date does not coincide with the date that the client requires, and the project has to be executed in a shorter timescale, then extra resources will be needed.

The most obvious choice of extra resource is Oliver, since he has the most to do on the critical chain. Oliver is the most over worked resources on the CC. Young could be an alternative.

So an additional resource is inserted into the programme and the above steps repeated, in this section 5.9, until the required completion date is achieved.

5.10 Managing the Buffers

Buffer management is one of the most important aspects of the critical chain project management.

The project leader is responsible for managing the project buffer, as he must ensure that the project is completed by the completion date.

This is a time risk management approach.
The buffer is divided into three sections—green, amber and red. The size of these divisions is up to the project manager and his judgement of the risks.

As tasks slip or are delayed, the project buffer is progressively used up. The rate of slippage into the project buffer is critical for completing the project on time.

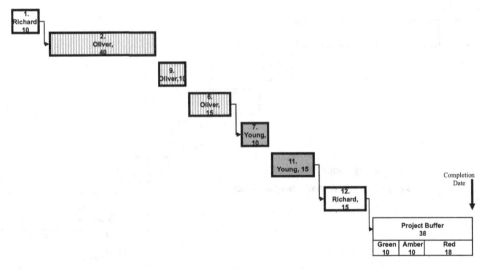

Fig 5.17 Project buffer divided into green, amber, red

Buffer management includes:
- o   If there is slippage into the green zone—just watch
- o   If this slippage persists into the amber zone—contingency plans must be prepared
- o   if slippage continues into the red zone—the contingency plans must be implemented

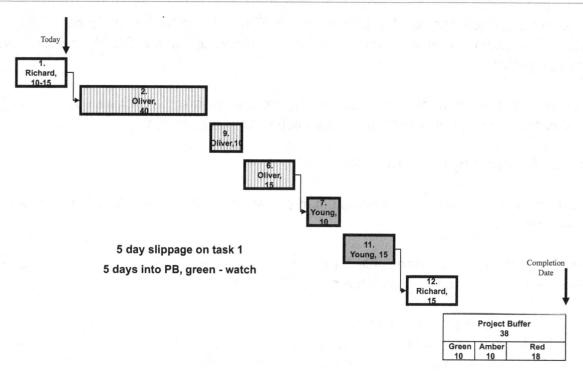

Fig 5.18 Task 1 has overrun, penetration into green zone of buffer—watch

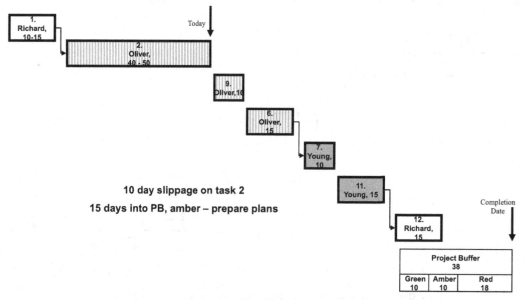

Fig 5.19 Task 2 has overrun, penetration into amber zone of buffer—produce contingency plans

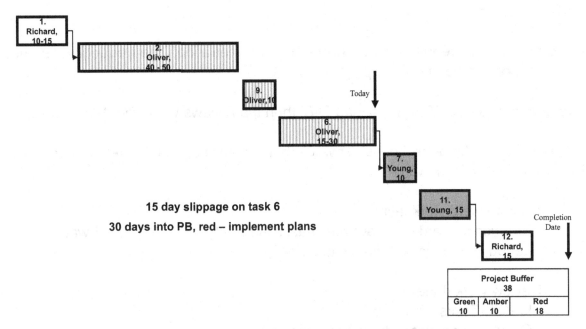

15 day slippage on task 6

30 days into PB, red – implement plans

Fig 5.20 Task 6 has overrun, penetration into the red zone— implement contingency plans

So the percentage of the project buffer used up is monitored against the overall percentage of the critical chain tasks. If the buffer is being used up at a greater rate than the completion of the tasks, there is a problem and action needs to be taken. The diagram below, Fig 5.21, is a way of tracking the buffer penetration during the life of the contract.

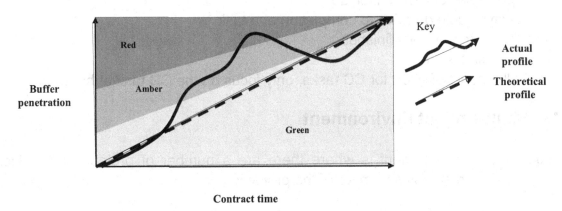

Fig 5.21 Buffer tracking showing penetration trends over time

The feeder buffers are managed in exactly the same way. If there are a large number of feeder buffers then the responsibility to manage the buffer penetration can be delegated to a manager responsible rather than the project leader.

Manage the buffers

Buffer reviews

There needs to be regular reviews of the buffer penetration. The frequency depends upon the size and nature of the project.

If your project is only 30days working 24/7 then the reviews would be daily.

If your project is 12months 5days per week then I would suggest the reviews are every 2 weeks with this framework:

- Issue forward work tasks
  - Produce forward list of activities/tasks in priority order, for next 3 week period, and check readiness to start

- Review work done
  - Identify Tasks completed
  - Outstanding tasks—duration to completion
  - Check actual work against planned progress, update fever chart, indicate buffer penetration and which zone, red, amber, green.
  - Identify what action to be taken to recover any overruns

- Delays
  - Record categories of any delay, reasons

The key principles of CCPM include
- Always quote duration to completion of a task
- Always report early finishes
- No multi-tasking
- Full amount of effort for CC tasks, only focus on the CC task at hand

5.11 Multi-Project Environment

A multi-project environment is where there are a number of projects with critical resources shared across a number of the projects.

In this case, each individual project will be managed as identified above. However, since the projects are connected by using, or sharing, the same resources, how do we ensure that there is no risk of any delay being transmitted from one project to another?

To overcome this, the critical resource across the projects is identified, since they are on the critical chain of the projects.

This critical resource becomes the "drum beat" of the business in that if their task is delayed, the whole business is affected. Their performance effectively determines the success of the business.

To minimise any transmission of delay from one project to another, a drum buffer is inserted at the point that this orange resource finishes their work on the first project and starts on the next project.

In multi-project environments, the role of the project manager becomes far less significant, particularly if there are a large number of projects e.g. in a design office. A lead designer could be the project manager for his design, and there will be a large number of lead designers all vying for resources. It is the Director's role to manage the critical resource (drum), that crosses all the projects, within that environment to ensure the best decisions are made overall.

5.12 Summary

Critical chain project management is a philosophy which includes the following six key stages:

- o Develop a logical traditional programme with estimated task duration that includes safety time, ensure resources are defined
- o Remove the safety time for the tasks
- o Remove any resource conflict
- o Identify the critical chain
- o Insert the project buffer and feeder buffers at strategic positions, with appropriate buffer sizes
- o Apply buffer management approach

This approach is about changing the culture of how we manage projects. If the attitude of the leader and project staff is not right then implementing this approach becomes very difficult. A specialist facilitator is recommended to help with any implementation.

5.13 Comparison between traditional project and Critical Chain Project Management

The table compares the behaviour of the traditional style of projects and the behaviour of critical chain style of projects.

Traditional Project Management	Critical Chain Project Management
Individual behaviour/culture Instinctively we avoid things damaging to us. Working for oneself, easy life. Blame culture.	**Individual behaviour/culture** Open and honest culture. Senior management as a role model. Working together. No blame.
CP Network planning. Estimate of task durations at low-risk to the person estimating, 80% probability. Critical Path	**CC Network planning.** Estimation of durations 50% probability. Network validation, task & resource definition. Identify the Critical Chain. Buffers included at strategic positions. Link project plans—"multi-project" environments.
Task Behaviour (execution) "Milestone" and date driven. Multi-tasking. "Urgent" task demand. Don't report early finishes.	**Task Behaviour (execution)** Only carry out planned tasks when required. Execute task as quickly as possible. No multi-tasking, staggering of projects. Report duration to completion. Report early finishes. Project and feeder buffer management -Green, amber, red buffers zones. -Contingency planning and implementation
Project Effects 80% missed original due date. 80% over original budget. cuts specification to bring back onto target time and cost. Fire fighting, crisis management. Low Morale. Changing priorities—gives a lack of sufficient and consistent focus. Lower margin than potential.	**Project Effects** On time, early if there is potential to come in 80% early without increasing resources. 80% within budget, controlled focus on where to spend additional money. To specification. Reduced overall working hours on project Better safety statistics. No, or reduced fire fighting. Higher morale. Significantly increased margin (2-3 times)
Business effects Uncompetitive thereby loss of future projects and market share. Turnover target not achieved. Profit target not achieved.	**Business effects** More competitive. Higher market share. Achieve turnover target. Achieve profit target.
Client effects Unhappy client. Award projects to competitors.	**Client effects** Happier client. Repeat business.

Chapter 5—The Best Project Performance

What have you discovered about project management?

How can you apply this to your projects?

What ideas has it given you to improve your project management?

What are some actions you can take to start managing your projects to achieve the best possible outcome?

1.

2.

3.

4.

5.

The Best Solution

6   The Best Solution

6.1   Existing problems

It is in the nature of projects to have difficulties, or problems, and include a number, or any combination, of the following:

- o   Performance issues
- o   Financial issues
- o   People issues
- o   Client issues
- o   Supply chain issues
- o   Management issues
- o   Leadership issues

These issues are either within the control/influence of the project leader or outside his control.

Often the project leader recognises many of these issues and puts a lot of effort into resolving many of them, particularly those which under his control. This effort is often spread over a number of improvements or initiatives. But does the issue go away, or does it get resolved briefly before it re-occurs? If this is the case, is the management effort well spent? Probably not.

This section is about a technique that will help provide the best solution with the least effort, and so least cost, to resolve internal issues.

The Best Solution, with the minimum of effort and at the least cost

---

6.2   New approach

Project management has been predominantly:

- o   Plan - plan and develop the programme
- o   Do - implement the plan or programme
- o   Check - review progress against the plan or programme

This follows closely the Deming cycle, Fig 6.1, which includes plan, do, check, act. The "act" is to take action to improve the way we do things.

If we are to achieve the best solution for the project, we have to expand this "plan, do, check, act" approach.

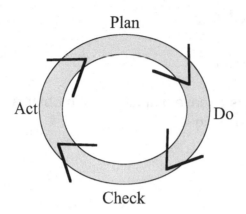

Fig 6.1 Deming cycle

The following problem solving approach, that all projects must employ, has been developed:

- Identify the symptoms
- Analyse the core issue
- Develop the direction of the solution
- Plan to implement the solution
- Implement the solution
- Check and monitor solution has been achieved

6.3   Identify the symptoms

All projects, by their nature, have difficulties. A key role of the project manger is to identify and resolve problems.

Identify the symptoms

How often do we put a solution into place to resolve a problem and then this problem comes back before too long? If this has happened, then there is another cause to the original problem that has not been resolved?

6.4   Analyse the core issue

Can all the project's problems, under the project leader's control be linked together to identify an underlying core issue? Fig 6.2.

Any external difficulties have to be analysed with the party involved, so these are dealt with separately. This analysis is therefore confined to what is within the project leader's control.

This core issue actually causes all the others, and is the constraint of the business. The constraint is holding the business back from performing more effectively.
This section is about constraint management.

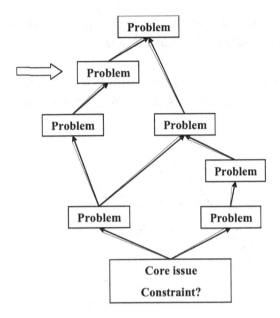

Fig 6.2 Core issue

If this core issue does exist, would it be important to identify and resolve it?

Yes it would, but in most cases solutions are implemented to solve "problems" on projects which are symptoms without the resolving of the core issue. Is this effort, time and cost, wasted? Would it be best to direct management time to identifying the core problem and resolving it?

So to get the best value solution, one that minimises effort and hence cost, but achieves the best result/outcome then we should focus our attention on the core issue, finding it and resolving it.

This is providing the best return on investment, the best value for money

Many managers and directors are reluctant to use this technique for reasons of internal fear. Fear that the issue will reflect themselves. So often the main driver of whether to use this technique or not, is their own view of themselves, and their fear, rather than their determination to achieve outstanding results.

Analyse the core issue, the best return on investment and value for money

This method of identifying the core issue was invented by Eli Goldratt and is widely explained in numerous books on the Theory of Constraints. This technique, with some adaptations, is describe here.

When difficulties occur with the operational performance, all these difficulties can be linked logically together to identify the core issue.

This core issue invariably lies with the senior management who, with the best will in the world, have not fully understood the effects of their policy decisions or way of thinking, Fig 6.3.

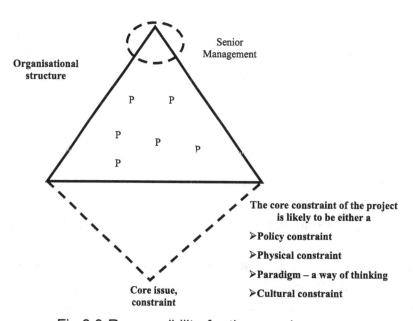

Fig 6.3 Responsibility for the core issue

The constraints are categorised as:-
- o Policy constraint
- o Physical constraint
- o Paradigm - a way of thinking
- o Culture constraint

6.5   Attitude

In order to apply this approach of finding the core issue of the project, the project leader must want to do it. The issues raised may be painful to the project leader, but if he has the right attitude and he wants to do the best for the project, he will be willing to carry out this type of analysis. So this requires immense courage and a strong internal belief of the project leader.

The analysis has to be carried out with the appropriate team members, in an environment of openness and honesty, to enable them to raise all the issues together and arrive at an agreed common issue, and agree the solution and way forward.

6.6   Analysis

Description of the analysis to find the core issue is as follows. A problem or an undesired outcome (UDO) has to be identified, which could be:
- Customer issues
- Operational performance issues
- Financial issues
- Strategic issues
- Cultural issues
- Team issues
- People issues
- Technology issues
- Research and Development issues

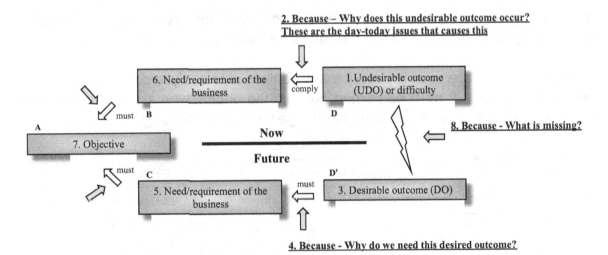

Fig 6.4 Conflict analysis (Eli Goldratt)

The above diagram, Fig 6.4, identifies the conflict between what we have now, box 1, and what we want in the future, box 3.

The conflict is that the desired outcome (DO), which is opposite of the undesired outcome (UDO), is not being achieved. Both sides of this conflict are trying to achieve the common objective.

The construction of this diagram must be carried out in sequence as follows, the numbers relate to the numbered boxes:

1. State what is the undesirable outcome (problem or difficulty)
2. Identify why this undesirable effect occurs. This is what is actually happening on a day to day basis. It could be related to the knowledge, attitude, achievements, skills, of the staff. It is essential to list all of the causes, even if there are many, and clarity is important. There will be a number of occurring themes.
3. State what is the desired outcome (opposite of box 1)
4. Identify why we need this desired outcome in box 3
5. Identify what business need is being satisfied by box 3.
6. Identify what business need is being satisfied that means we comply with box 1 (this is the hardest box to understand on the diagram)
7. Define what is the common objective from both sides of this diagram. This will be some simple statement that describes success.
8. List out what is missing that stops us from overcoming the list from box 2 and thereby move us from box 1 to achieve box 3 (again list all of the themes that have been identified, they are likely to be something that has not been clearly defined and issued)

In order to ensure this analysis works, there needs to absolute clarity of the statements made, the greater the clarity the more robust the analysis.

This approach can be used to describe any conflict, or to analyse core problems of the project or part of it. It must be carried out with the people who are involved and any decision maker, in order to get them to change their understanding.

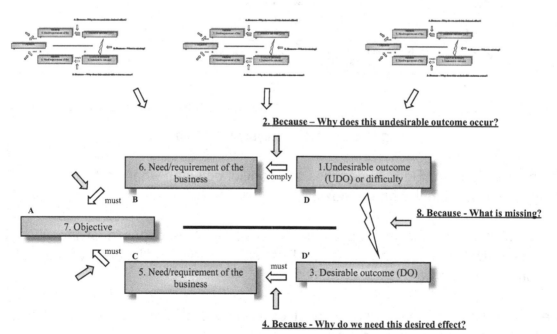

Fig 6.5 Example of a Conflict analysis

An example of this diagram is given in Fig 6.5. This is a real example of an analysis for an audit function within a project, whereby the internal audit report was not produced on time. All of the statements in box 8 were the responsibilities of the audit manager, and she asked "is this my role?". She had been recently put into the manager's role without any understanding of that was required as a manager.

The following statement was produced that summaries the issues in box 8 and was considered to be a core issue of the audit function:

> "The internal audits are not planned with a clear scope, timescale, resources, guidance, evidence requirements and reviews, which is agreed and communicated with those involved"

6.7   Three problem analysis

As the heading suggests, in order to identify the core problem of the project, three significant problems, from the same project, that are under the influence of the project leader, are analysed.

For each of these three problems the above problem analysis is carried out in turn. With the three diagrams defined there will be common trends or similarities which appear in boxes 8.

These three diagrams are then summarised into one composite diagram as shown, Fig 6.6.

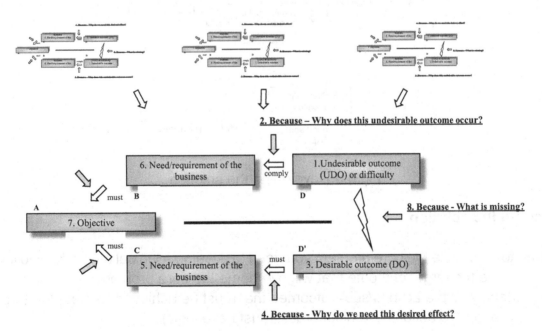

Fig 6.6 Three problem composite diagram

6.8   Construction of the Composite diagram

The construction of the composite diagram must follow the numbering sequence, 7,5,3,6,1,8. It identifies what is the common statement that links the same boxes from the three individual analyses in to the corresponding numbered box in the composite diagram.

There are likely to be a statements in box 8 of the composite diagram which identify all the things that are missing from the previous 3 problem analysis diagrams.

These statements can be summarised as a single element that is missing in the business. This is the core problem and often relates to something strategic which is the responsibility of a senior manager.

6.9   Develop the solution

To overcome the core problem, there has to be a target, normally it's the positive version of the core problem. Having identified the target/outcome, then the actions/tasks can be identified to achieve it.

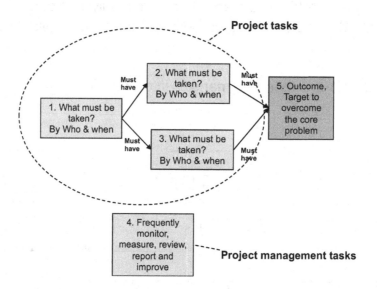

Fig 6.6 Developing the solution

Planning the solution

To plan to overcome the core problem you need to develop a logical diagram as follows:
- o   Agree the target/outcome that will overcome the core problem
- o   Identify all the actions/sub-outcomes that must be achieved to meet the target
- o   Arrange the actions in logical order (must have logic)
- o   Identify responsibilities for carrying these actions

- o Identify the timescales
- o Agree the measures of success and reviews

This in itself becomes a project with a defined target or outcome, a logical diagram, a project leader, with responsibilities and timescale.

With a trained facilitator then the above stages, of carrying out the core problem analysis and develop the solution, could be completed in a workshop lasting half a day.

A detailed plan or programme may be needed, with dates and responsibilities for delivery of actions. Measures will be needed that demonstrate a success outcome.

The project team that are needed to implement the solution are then identified and briefed on the project, and are allocated roles and tasks.

Also, how the achievement of this plan will be measured, monitored and reviewed to ensure the deadlines are achieved, will need to be defined.

Develop the solution

Implementing the solution

The project team implements the plan or programme to the agreed timescale.

Implement the solution

Achievement of the tasks and outcome need to be regularly monitored, measured, reviewed, and action to improve performance to ensure that the solution is achieved.

This approach has been used to analyse numerous businesses, organisations and projects, with no prior knowledge of that business, and still arrived at the core issue of that business within a few hours.

Check, monitor, review and improve until the solution is implemented

---

Chapter 6—The Best Solution

What have you discovered about project management?

How can you apply this to your projects?

What ideas has it given you to improve your project management?

What are some actions you can take to start managing your projects to achieve the best possible outcome?

1.

2.

3.

4.

5.

The Best Project Leader

7 The Best Project Leader

If the project to achieve the best outcome then the project leader has to achieve all of the above, sections 3 to 6. This is a daunting task.

7.1 Strong leadership

The project leader, of any size of project, plays a vital role in achieving its outcome. If the project has the wrong leader then its full potential will not be realised.

As Norman Haste, Chief Operating Officer, Laing O'Rourke Middle East Operations, says:

"Projects never fail because of technical input; they fail because of lack of leadership"

If the full potential of the project, and hence the best outcome, is to be achieved then the right leader has to be appointed for the required role. He has to have the right personality, the right profile, the right skills for the project context discussed in section 2.

For complex projects, strong leadership is always needed.

If the right leader cannot be found, as is often the case, then this must be recognised and the Board Director needs to take action to compensate.

7.2 Role

The role of the project leader will depend on the size and complexity of the project, section 2. A simple project may just be task orientated and the project leader's role would be to complete the tasks.

However, for a large project, the leader's role becomes far more complex and involved, as described below.

Direction, strategic thinking and project strategy

The project leader's main role is to define the direction, strategic thinking of the project, produce the project strategy, as discussed in section 3, and keep it up to date in line with any changes in strategic thinking and the needs of the client.

Having developed the strategy he has to communicate it so that all project team members are fully aware of the project, its purpose, vision, outcome, timescale, logical plan.

The project leader must clearly define the outcome and purpose of each team and align that team to the direction of the project.

The project leader must ensure that each team member has their own outcome and purpose for their role, aligned to the team's outcome and purpose.

He should be continuously reinforcing and communicating what is in the project strategy and its principles and values.

The project leader is also responsible for completing the project successfully and ensuring it is seen to be a success in the eyes of his client and Board Director.

Client's and Board Director needs

The project leader has to continuously understand his client and Board Director's needs, as discussed in section 3, and ensure these needs are met.

It is what the Client and Board Director says to promote the project that determines how successful the project is.

Motivating the project staff and supply chain

In order to complete the project successfully, the project leader has to align his staff and the supply chain to the project strategy, understand their needs, and support and motivate them. This is discussed in section 4.

Managing the project

The project leader has overall responsibility for completing the project on time, to cost and to quality.
He has to:
  o Monitor performance, update the measurement systems and KPIs
  o Produce reports on the project performance and KPIs
  o Hold regular meetings to review progress
  o Implement improvement actions and plans to overcome any delays
  o Communicate performance to the project staff and other key stakeholders
  o Ensure that the Client and Board Director are satisfied

7.3   Personal values

The project leader will need to align his own personal values with the values that he is trying to create for the project.

If he is to be really motivated himself, his career aspirations and what he wants to achieve in life, have to be aligned with achieving project success. If he can see that there will be no advancement, having successfully completed the project, then he won't put in the extra effort that will be needed to achieve the best possible outcome.

He needs to be really passionate and loves what he is doing.

A strong leader should have values such as:
- Positive, future focused
- Enthusiastic, passionate
- Committed, focused
- Leading by example, role model

He needs to create an environment that enables the project team to work well together, giving their best, to achieve a successful project outcome.

These values have been produced diagrammatically, Fig 7.1, showing those values that are internal to the project leader, those that are external within the project environment that he has to create to enable his project staff to achieve their best, thereby achieving the best possible outcome.

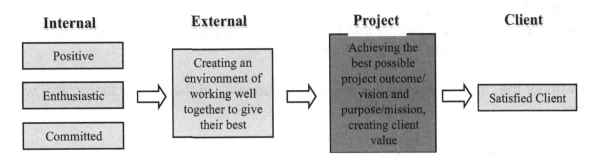

Fig 7.1 Project Leader's Values

7.4 Attributes

To achieve the above values, an effective leader of a complex project needs to:
- o be a decisive decision-maker, with persistence, and tenacity
- o have humanity, humility, selflessness, self-sacrifice, empathy
- o have humour, self-awareness, understanding, moral principles.
- o be creative, innovative, imaginative, inventive, flexible
- o understand, decide, communicate, delegate, inspire, and achieve
- o passionate and loves his role

Above all he must be respected and trusted and have respect and trust. He must have high moral principles. Everything he does must be for the best of the project.

He needs to concern himself with the whole life development of his project staff, both in and out of work.

True leaders have a **presence**, this is the ability to influence others. People take notice and are influenced by them and, without this, they will not become true leaders.

7.5   Profile

The project leader's own profile must fit the profile of the role, as described in section 2. Different project sizes and levels of complexity will require different profiles for the project leader.

There have been many complex projects in which the project leader was either: past orientated, he was comfortable in the ways that he had used in the past; or present oriented, his focus was on today's tasks, or this week's tasks, or this month's tasks; rather than the future of the project, focusing on the project outcomes.

If the leader is past focused he will struggle to understand what he has to do long-term for the future, he does not develop the required approaches. As a result, the project will struggle to perform and develop.

This is called the "Law of the Lid" whereby the project will not develop beyond the capabilities of the top person, as that top person will always act as a brake to prevent things developing outside his comfort zone.

So without the match between the role and personality of the leader, the project will suffer.

7.6   Behaviour

People believe in the person first and then the message and what he is saying.

People believe in the person first and then the message

When a client is meeting a project leader for the first time, then within 60 seconds, he forms an impression. That impression comes from the leader's non-verbal messages, his behaviour, his own internal belief system.

This impression will stay with the client for a long-time.

So behaviour and body language are crucially important.

Non-Verbal messages

If the client is going to believe in the project leader's ability to deliver the non-verbal messages from the project leader have to be right.

- o Physiology - his body language has to be positive, forward, confident, determined
- o Focus - he focuses on the future, forward, can do attitude, determined
- o Language - his language that he uses has to have energy, enthusiasm, determination with the right tone
- o Image - he needs to look the part, professional
- o Relationships - he is able to get on with the key stakeholders

Role Model

Since people often reflect the behaviour of their manager, the project leader must behave in the way he wants his team to behave.

So the project leader must be the right role model. He must portray his values, positive, enthusiastic and commitment all the time.

He must also create the right environment for the project team to work well together, and give their best. He must understand the different personalities and any friction, be able to resolve these and put his staff in roles that suit their personalities best.

Encouragement

He must give praise when it is due, but the praise must be heartfelt. He must also reward teams for exceptional performance. Above all he must fully support and encourage his team.

Challenging

He must continuously challenge his team to achieve their best performance by asking open questions, such as:
- How can you do that better?
- How quick can you achieve this?
- What is the best possible time you can do this in"
- What else can you do?

By challenging his team he is getting them to realise that doing things differently is accepted, taking safe risks. The project leader will then be motivating his staff. And by doing this he will be getting them to innovate, to improve, to grow and understand better ways.

Above all the team members will perform better and deliver their best performance with will benefit the project's performance.

Image

The project leader must look the part, he must have a positive image. It is often first impressions that count.

If he wants to portray a professional approach then he has to look and behave in a professional way.

7.7   Belief

Internal belief

To do all of this, the project leader must have a strong belief of himself.

But what is the Project Leader selling? The project leader has been contracted to provide a product, a service, results or a benefit to a client, but what is it that he is actually selling to the client?

He is not selling a product, service, result or benefit. He is selling a belief. The client has to believe that he, as the project leader with his project team, can, will and are delivering their best performance.

When the project leader is dealing with the client, then he has to sell himself, and his belief, so that the client believes the leader, the project and the team.

If this is done successfully then the client will promote the project, and there will be a perception that the best outcome is being achieved irrespective of the actual performance.

The project leader is selling a belief within himself

So project leadership is about selling that belief and managing the relationship with his client, and with his Board Director.

Managing these relationships is managing their belief in his ability.

To do this, the project leader has to believe in himself, understand himself, his weaknesses, strengths and believe in his own, and his team's abilities to do their best.

The project leader has to have a strong belief in what he is saying, in his ability and in what he can do. He mustn't pretend. The project leader must be honest, must take praise and blame, be interested in the client, in his Board Director and all the people around him.

If he believes he can achieve, and values himself, he must have positive energy, his body language must be positive, must be cheerful, pleasant and happy. He must focus on the positive, he must be upbeat, enthusiastic and optimistic, and have a can-do attitude. He must always be realistic.

The project leader believes within himself

Belief in his team

He must believe in other people, in his team and their abilities. He must forget any mistakes that they have made, it's history, it is in the past. He must be interested in others to give genuine empathy, and be really patient. He must always focus on what is required for the future.

Team commitment

If the project leader takes time, if he is interested and he listens to his team, he will get the commitment that he is after. It is only by getting this commitment that he is going to get the best out of his people.

Interest and patience will earn him the commitment of the staff.

7.8   Principles

So the behaviour of the project leader is essential for the best possible outcome. But above all, the project leader must adhere to his core values, ethics and principles.

Everything that he, and the team, do must be done for the project, and hence for the client, it must be for the right principles and be ethical.

7.9   Trust

The project leader must be trustworthy to create trust within the client and his team. He must always do what he says he will do, he must be trustworthy.

If there is a lack of trust, then this is the route to failure in the relationship, and hence the profitability of the project. So, trustworthiness of the project leader is crucial.

It is only through trust that the project can succeed.

Above all, a project leader has to listen to the client. It is really important that he listens and understands, and develops that rapport with the client, which will then build on the trust. This trust will become the basis of success.

He must do what he says he will do. He has to keep his promises, and his commitments, to develop integrity and become trustworthy. When he expresses his feelings, he has got to express them with the right intent, with the right positive outcome, and not blaming.

He has to balance the feelings and convictions of others to be able to energise his staff, and enable them to be creative, even when he has to give negative feedback.

The project leader always achieves enthusiasm and creativity within people

---

7.10   Own vision and core values

If the project leader believes in his own vision of what he wants to achieve in his business life, and why, with his core values, and if they are all aligned to delivering the project, you are going to get a lot more out of that project leader.

He must set compelling vision and purpose, future outcomes for the project and communicate these to his team. He has to ensure that his team fully buy-into them.

We have discussed the planning for the project leader, designing the role and finding the right person for the personality profile at the various stages of the project, and the behaviour of the project leader. These are all hugely important elements of project management and are often overlooked.

How important is the project leader in achieving the project's full potential?

If the project leader himself isn't happy in what he is doing, and doesn't particularly like leading this particular project, and his own emotional personal needs are not being satisfied, or he doesn't feel he is being supported by his bosses, then he will not perform as well as he could. Also the project staff and client will unconsciously pick up this doubt and be affected by it.

So to get the best out of the project leader, then his personal needs have to be identified and met.

7.11   Managing the Key stakeholders

For the key stakeholders, client and Board Director, to say that the project is successful, the project leader must ensure their motivational needs are satisfied.

There is a lot resting on the project leader. He has to convince himself, convince the client, convince the Board, convince the key supply chain and also convince his own project staff that he, with the team, can deliver the project.

Also, the project leader must be able to give the client the variety of options, the choices, the key decisions that the client needs to make. He needs to make sure the client is sufficiently involved in the decision making him feel part of the process.

The project leader first listens and understands, then to be understood

---

The project leader must make the client feel significant, and that his ideas are important. The project leader must listen to the client, first to understand, and then to be understood. The client always has good ideas and the project leader has to listen to them and take them on board if necessary, or to develop the client's ideas into a practical solution. The client mustn't feel that he is being ignored or undermined.

The project leader has to have a close rapport with the client as if they are friends. The project leader may or may not like the client as a person, but it is up to the project leader to get on well with the client.

The project leader has to gain the client's trust, so he has to understand where he is coming from, he has to understand quite a bit about the client's background, family life, particular interests so that they can talk freely together.

The project leader must be able to get the client to grow, to learn, to develop, to understand more, so the project leader in some sense becomes the client's teacher.

So, the project leader has to make sure the client feels able to contribute to the success of the project, to the success of the project leader and to the success of the project team. And again, the client must feel that he is valuable to the project, that he has a contribution to make, and that the project leader values him.

If the client feels personally involved with the project, knows what is happening and believes in the ability of the project leader and his team, and feels involved with the key decision making, then he will promote the project.

Client promotes the project, it is achieving its potential

The whole purpose of the project leader's role is to get the client to say "yes, this project has achieved its full potential—it's achieved the best possible outcome". This is the generic definition of success of any project.

To achieve this then the personal emotional needs of the client have to be fully satisfied, section 3.

These six human needs can be addressed during every dealing between the project leader and the client:

- face to face discussions
- on the phone
- by email
- by letter

With every interaction with the client, the project leader must be fully aware of whether he is hitting all of these six human needs or not.

Client's six human needs continually satisfied

All it takes is one careless word and trust can go immediately. It takes a long time for that trust to re-establish itself, so the role of the project leader and the relationship he has with the client is so important.

If the relationship isn't succeeding between the project leader and the client, there may be different beliefs and values, or their emotional needs may not be fully satisfied.

If the project leader really wants to make a relationship work, the values and human needs must be satisfied.

Project with common beliefs and values

The role of the project leader is so important, that if the project leader doesn't get it right, if his beliefs are wrong, if his values are wrong or if he doesn't meet the six human needs of the client, his team, his Board Director, or the supply chain, the best possible outcome will not be achieved.

The first set of project leader's needs, identified below, is how much authority he has in carrying out his role.

	The Project Leader's Role
Certainty	1. That he has the resources needed to deliver the project outcome 2. He has the trust and confidence of his Director
Choice	1. He has the freedom to make his own decisions
Significance	1. His role is important to the business 2. He is important to the business
Connection, Rapport	1. He has the support of his Board Director, they listen to him 2. He has the support of his team, they listen to him
Growth	1. He is learning and that the project will do him good 2. He will get recognition, there is a benefit to him
Contribution	1. He contributes to the success of the client, the business, Board Director, 2. He contributes to the success of the project, staff, and himself

The second set of needs is internal, it is inner self-belief. It is this self-belief that will provide his confidence, and the belief that his Director and client will have in him.

	The Project Leader's belief in himself
Certainty	1. He believes in his own abilities, he is confident 2. He believes in his knowledge, his management approach, his people skills, his technical understanding
Choice	1. He believes that he has a number of options to decide from 2. He believes that he can find solutions
Significance	1. He believes that his approach is important 2. He believes that what he can offer is important
Connection, Rapport	1. He believes that he can develop the necessary close relationships 2. He believes that he can listen to and understand the client and Board Director
Growth	1. He believes he can learn new ways 2. He believes he is open to new suggestions
Contribution	1. He believes he can contribute to the success of the client 2. He believe he contribute to the success of the project and the business

If the project leader portrays a strong inner belief, then the client will believe in him

The project leader's belief in himself will be self-evident automatically, it cannot be disguised. If he is not confident himself, this will become evident within the non-verbal language.

- o Physiology - his body language has to be positive, forward, confident, determined
- o Focus - he focuses on the future, forward, can do attitude, determined
- o Language - his language that he uses has to have energy, enthusiasm, determination with the right tone
- o Image - he needs to look the part, professional
- o Relationships - he is able to get on with the key stakeholders

---

People believe in the person first before the message

The project leader plays a vital role in ensuring that the client believes that team are doing their best to achieve the project outcome.

If the project leader does not believe in himself, the client will pick this up immediately through non-verbal signs.

Often project success is not the delivery of the project to time, cost and quality, even though these elements are hugely important. Success, in the eyes of the client, often depends on whether the client believes that the project leader and the project team have done their best to achieve the best possible outcome.

So the belief that the client has will determine how successful the project is from the client's perspective. And managing this belief within the client is an essential aspect of the project leader's role.

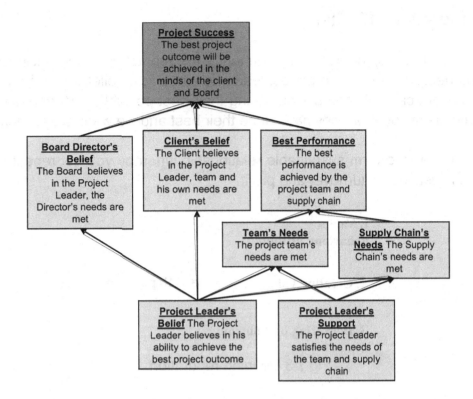

Fig 7.2 Project leader's belief is the root of success

This diagram, Fig 7.2, indicates that if the project leader believes in himself, he will engender the client and Board Director's belief in him. If the project leader satisfies the needs of the team and the supply chain, the best possible performance is likely to be achieved.

This best possible performance, coupled with the belief in the project leader, will mean the client and the Board Director will see the project as a success.

The Project Leader must believe in himself to achieve project success

The project leader has to satisfy the emotional needs of the client. He has to understand what will give the client certainty of the project, certainty of the outcome, certainty of the project leaders' ability to achieve it, and the certainty of the project team to achieve the outcome

The Project Leader is selling a belief within himself

7.12 Reputation (4CFQs)

A key focus of the project leader is to enhance the reputation of the business during the project delivery. Hence the project leader is creating a belief within the client that he and his team can, will and are delivering their best possible performance. Hoping to make the client say that "they have done their best and we want to use them again".

So success is a long-term sustainable relationship whereby you get repeat business which gives sustainable turnover and profit.

1. Values
Behaviour, attitude

+

2. Creating Value   =   **Reputation**

+

3. Delivering best outcome

Fig 7.3 Defining reputation

Fig 7.3 Show the 3 elements that make up your project's reputation. We have already covered values and delivering the best possible outcome. So here we will cover how do we create value for your client?

We often use the phrase "create value" but what does this mean?

Our client's are expecting us to deliver time, cost and quality, it is what we have been contracted to achieve. And this is measured at the end of the project, was it on-time, within budget and to the required standards?

Creating value is done throughout the project life, it is every day, week, month. It is continuous.

Understanding how to create client value is through the following 4 Client Focused questions (4CFQs). These are:

1. What is most important to you about the service we are providing to you? - this is what is valuable to the client - values
2. Why is this most important to you? - beliefs
3. How can I best serve you in meeting these needs?—best/excellence
4. How would you measure whether the service I provide to you is excellent? - measure

These questions can be applied at 3 levels in your business.

1. If your business is in a long-term relationship with your client doing many projects, then the CEOs can get-together and these questions asked. The answers, values, will be of strategic importance to your client and they should then be formally published.

2. When awarded a project, then your project leader should ask the same questions of the client's representation for the project. These client values for the project should then be circulated and followed by the senior management team.

3. On a large project if your client has a senior management team that mirrors your senior management team, then each of your managers can ask the same question of their counterparts. These are then the aspects that the manager must always focus on when interfacing with their counterparts.

If your business wants to change the reputation that it has, then they must define what they want to be known for, their desired reputation, and then ensure these values are followed throughout the project. Sooner or later this reputation would have been established.

7.13 Creating success

Fig 7.3 is a future reality tree that shows how to create success.

It starts of with understanding and creating client values, defining the project direction and defining and behaving in line with our values.

Then, if the best performance is achieved in everything we do (including every interaction with the client), and if we continuously demonstrate this (formal and informal demonstration), and the client believes us, then the client will believe that we have done our best to deliver the best possible out come.

They are then likely to want to use us again, there will be a long-term relationship, and we will get repeat business thereby helping towards long-term sustainable business and profit.

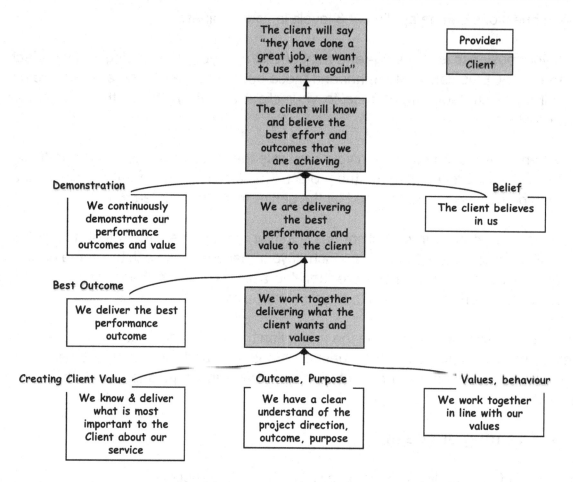

Fig 7.3 Creating success

7.14 High performing teams

There are 4 aspects in creating a high performing team.
These include:
1. the team members need to be passionate about what they do, they need to be enthusiastic, committed and believe in the project and themselves.
2. the team need to have clarity of the direction they are going in, the 4Qs have been defined, including outcome and purpose.
3. the client needs must be clear, also how to create client value, 4CFQs
4. above all the team must deliver excellence at all times with every contact with the client

If this is provided within the 5PM framework for your project, then you will have a high performing team.

If this approach can be replicated by all the teams on your project, strategic team, tactical teams operational teams, and any functional teams then your project performance will surpass any performance that you have had so far. You will achieve exceptional results.

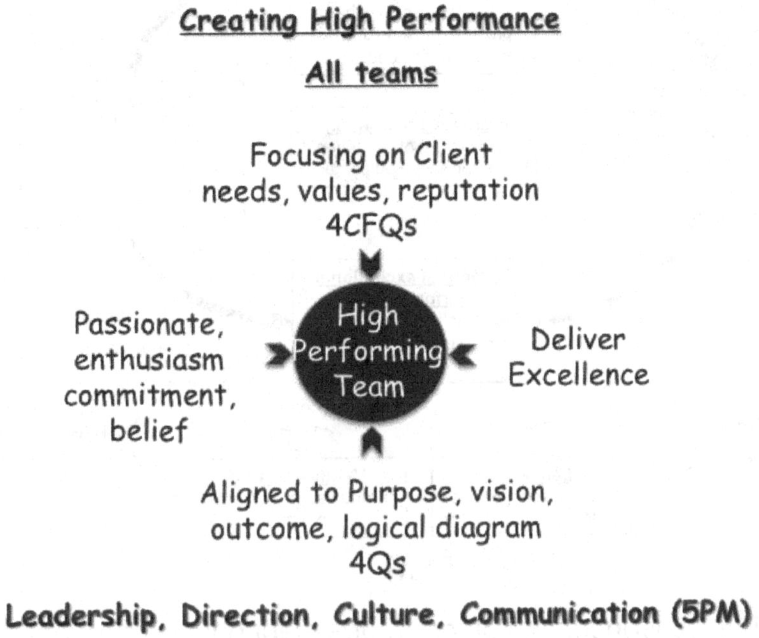

Creating High Performance

All teams

Focusing on Client
needs, values, reputation
4CFQs

Passionate,
enthusiasm
commitment,
belief

High
Performing
Team

Deliver
Excellence

Aligned to Purpose, vision,
outcome, logical diagram
4Qs

Leadership, Direction, Culture, Communication (5PM)

Fig 7.4 High performing teams

7.15. Creating Exceptional Performance

Achieving exceptional performance can be achieved for any business with the openness and commitment of the senior management using the 5PM, 4Qs and 4CFQs. You must have the best team leader and team to ensure that it works.

This has been the main basis of this book and is summarised below, Fig 7.5.

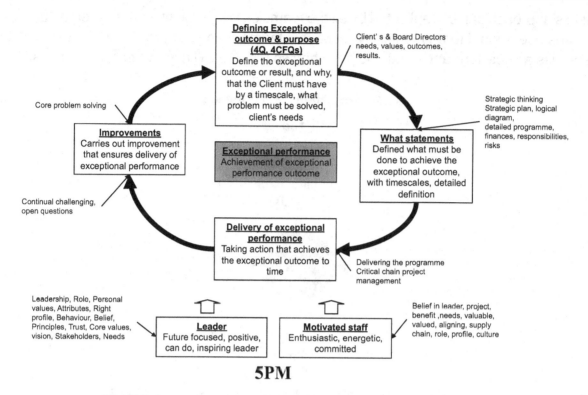

Fig 7.5 Conceptual diagram of exceptional performance

If this diagram is followed, using the appropriate techniques in this book, then the best possible outcome and exceptional performance will be achieved.

Chapter 7—The Best Project Leader

What have you discovered about project management?

How can you apply this to your projects?

What ideas has it given you to improve your project management?

What are some actions you can take to start managing your projects to achieve the best possible outcome?

1.

2.

3.

4.

5.

8   Implementation

8.1   Getting started

In order to gain confidence that these techniques do work and exceptional results can be achieved then it is best to try them out on an initial team.

Choose a smallish team with an enthusiastic team leader and team members. The project sponsor must (4Qs):
1. Define their outcome that they must deliver by a certain date
2. Define what the compelling reason is for delivering this outcome by that date. It is this purpose that creates the energy, so it needs to be compelling. Also define the benefits that the achievement of this outcome will bring to the business. Define success.
3. Define the problem that must be resolved by the team.
   Then get the team together, explain the above, and then get them to:
4. Define what has to have been done that will deliver the outcome/purpose and overcome the problem. This is the logical diagram.

Get the team to define who their key clients/customers are, internal or external. The define what is important to them (4CFQs). Also do this for each team member and their client/customers.

Then
- Allocate each sub-outcome on the logical diagram to a team member.
- Agree the best timescale that these sub-outcomes can be completed by.
- Get each team member to list out the specific actions that they will take, and by when, to deliver their sub-outcome. If necessary convert into a detailed programme.

Then agree regular review meeting dates for the review of the actions and completion of the sub-outcomes and actions to overcome any slippages.

During the implementation of the actions create an environment of continuously challenging the team members, with open questions, thereby encouraging innovation/ improvements and hence the best performance is achieved.

Also ensure the client/customer values are always satisfied during implementation, comes from the 4CFQs.

You may find that, during the implementation, existing systems, processes, procedures are hindering performance. Then you have to decide whether they:

a. are important as they are legal, industry, contract related and cannot be modified, and therefore must be followed
b. can be modified, or ignored, to allow the project actions to progress

When success has been achieved then this approach can be rolled out to other teams, one by one.

8.2   How can a CEO implement these techniques?

First of all produce guidance notes on the application 5PM that all teams are expected to follow.

1. Director level—Reporting the CEO

The CEO should get all his Directors, reporting to him, to define (4Qs) for their department/function:
1. What must they achieve? Their strategic outcome, by when
2. Why must they achieve it? Their strategic purpose.
3. What must they have achieved that will deliver the outcome? Their Logical Diagram.
4. What the problem is that they must overcome, or their opportunity.

(Note: "outcomes" and "sub-outcomes" are what the business requires to be achieved by that team, these strategic outcomes/sub-outcomes must be delivered by a particular timescale to be successful, this is the definition of success from the client's and shareholder's perspective)

When each of the Directors have defined their 4Qs above, then ensure there is full agreement that, collectively, these outcomes and purposes will deliver the vision of the business.

All these outcomes & purposes must be linked into delivering an improved service, greater productivity, satisfying current clients, new markets/clients, product development and speed to market.

The timescale by which the strategic outcome must be delivered should be agreed.

Get the Directors to define who their customers are (could be internal customers or external clients), and what is important to them (4CFQs)

Strategic reviews are then agreed, the frequency, attendees, purpose, agenda. This is the achievement of the strategic outcomes and what needs to be done to ensure delivery.

All decisions, processes, procedures, behaviours, actions must then be aligned to delivering their purpose (for each strategic team and for the business as a whole).

Then define what the Directors behaviour needs to be like, e.g. passionate, committed, future focused, challenging, understanding, listening, supporting, consistent. They must agree to follow these values and behaviours from then on.

Each Director must write all the above down and produce their strategic document by which their team, and sub-teams, will be managed—their compelling purpose, outcome, problem or opportunity, logical diagram (4Qs) customer/client values/beliefs (4CFQs), behaviour/values.

This will include the outcome and compelling purpose for each of their teams and the timescale by which these outcomes must be achieved.

2. Management Level—managers reporting to each Director

Each manager must agreed, with their Director, the outcome and compelling purpose for each of their teams under their authority, with timescales. This must be linked back to the Director's strategic direction.

Each manager leading must bring together each team (4Qs):
1. Confirm their outcome that has been set for them
2. Confirm their compelling purpose that has been set for them
3. Define what must they have achieved that will deliver the outcome? Their own team's logical diagram.
4. What the problem is that they must overcome, or their opportunity.

Define the 4CFQs for their team.

The manager's reviews with their team are then agreed, the frequency, attendees, purpose, agenda. This is the achievement of the outcomes and what needs to be done to ensure delivery.

3. Operational level—team members reporting to the manager

The sub-outcomes within the team's logical diagram are then allocated to a team member (or could be another sub-team), with timescales.

This sub-outcome needs to form part of their job description, get the team member to updated their job description with their sub-outcome and compelling purpose.

The team member must list out all the specific actions that are needed to deliver their sub-outcome.

4. Process (operational)

If the team member's sub-outcome is still complex and involves a number of people then a process could be produced.

The process definition needs to include:
1. Overall responsibility, this is the team member
2. Process's outcome
3. Process's compelling purpose
4. How is the outcome/purpose to be measured
5. The process flow
6. The process input and output
7. Responsibilities for actions within the flow

Leaders—(CEO, Directors, Managers, Team Leaders)

All leaders must fit their role. They must have the required experience, knowledge, competency, personality, character, communications skills, ability to provide direction, supportive of their team, be a role model, and have the right profile for their role.

Values and Behaviour—culture

All staff, and in particular the leaders of the business, need to exhibit the right behaviours. These are the values and behaviours that are defined, in writing, by the CEO and Directors. These must be cascaded down and all staff informed. The leaders must be role models and ensure these values and behaviour are instilled at all times.

Team Members

All leaders must be supporting of their team members. When they have set the direction of their team, outcome and compelling purpose, then they must align their them members to that direction e.g. each team member has a sub-outcome.

The team members are then continually challenged to deliver their outcome faster, better by asking open questions.

Also the team members must feel valued and valuable by having their 6 emotional needs met. The team leader must spend time with each team member to listen and understand their issues, the team leader must provide support and direction to get their commitment.

Challenging

It is essential that a challenging culture is created. The reason for this is 2 fold
1. to ensure the right clarity of outcome, purpose and sub-outcome
2. by asking open questions to challenge each team member to deliver their personal outcome faster, better, cheaper (without compromising safety, quality)

Chapter 8—Implementation

What have you discovered about project management?

How can you apply this to your projects?

What ideas has it given you to improve your project management?

What are some actions you can take to start managing your projects to achieve the best possible outcome?

1.

2.

3.

4.

5.

Summary

9 Summary of the 5 project management techniques (5PM)

PM Basics

These are the basics of project management that are essential for all projects and include:
- o Integration management
- o Scope management
- o Time management
- o Cost management
- o Quality management
- o Risk management
- o HR management
- o Procurement management
- o Communication management
- o Stakeholder management

These are currently taught and applied to projects. However, 80% of projects worldwide fail to be delivered to time, cost and quality or scope has to be cut to bring the project back on track.

Therefore, the way project are currently being taught and managed is insufficient. So what additional techniques are needed that will guarantee the best outcome of the project will be obtained?

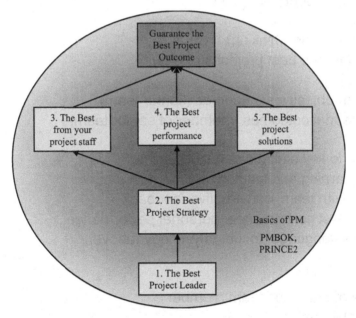

Fig 9.1 The 5 project management techniques to guarantee success, (5PM)

The following is a summary of the 5PM techniques that are crucial to "Guaranteeing the Best Possible Outcome" for you project.

The Best Project Leader (Complex Projects)

1. Personality (charismatic)
   - Language
     - "will do, can do" attitude
     - Passion in voice, energy, tone
     - Express confidence
   - Focus
     - Future
     - Always forward looking
   - Physiology (right image—how he looks)
     - Open body language
     - Standing straight up, head up, looking straight and up
     - Smiling, laughing, fun

2. Character
   - Beliefs
     - Strong self belief, and belief in staff
   - Values
     - Achievement, professionalism, openness, people do their best
     - Supporting, trusting integrity
   - Principles
     - Right intent for project (not self)

3 Direction/Strategy (future thinking)
   - Strategic plan (the best project strategy)
   - Future thinking
   - Setting team objectives/outcomes (senior team)
   - Setting personal outcomes (member of senior team)

4 Communication (to key stakeholders)
   - Listening, learning and leading
   - Discussion with team, constructive feedback
   - Verbal—project performance, personal performance
   - Non-verbal—language, focus, physiology (above)

5 Supportive
   - Supportive of team and team member
   - Creating cohesion
   - Challenging
   - Open questions

6 Culture
- o Creating the right culture, based upon the right values and behaviour
- o Acting as a role model

The Best Project Strategy

1. Project context

2. Defined 4Qs of project management,
   - outcome, and timescale to be delivered
   - purpose, why does the outcome have to be delivered
   - problem to overcome,
   - what has to be in place, logical diagram, timescale

3. Defined scope, deliverables, success definition

4. Stakeholders
   - o client needs, values, 4CFQs
   - o other stakeholders and end user requirements

5. Defined resource plan and responsibilities on logical plan
   - o Resource Plan, numbers, skills/competencies
   - o Organisational chart, reporting lines
   - o Roles and responsibilities linked to logical plan including:
     - Project Sponsor, Project Leader, Project Team Members

6. Defined detailed programme, if required, derived from logical plan

7. Defined financial plan for project duration
   - o Budget profile
   - o Cost forecast profile
   - o Cost actual profile

8. Risk and Benefits
   - o Non achievement of outcomes on logical diagram
   - o Other risk that may effect the project from external sources

9. Measurement—KPI
   - o Linked to outcomes on logical diagram
   - o Financial and performance

10. Processes if required
    - o e.g. change control, approvals, handover, interface processes

11. Communications plan, how formal communications will work, purpose
    o Team, Client, Project sponsor
    o Purpose, style/format, frequency

12. Monitoring, measuring reviewing and improving meetings
    o Purpose and agenda, dates, frequencies, attendees
    o Measures, monitoring, actions

13. Culture
    o Values, behaviours, attitudes

Define all above in a strategy document, which is then signed and approved by sponsor. It is then communicated to the project team in the start up meeting, and to other interested parties.

The Best from your Staff

Your project staff need to
- Belief in the project leader
- Belief in the project
- Belief that they themselves benefit

Their own emotional needs are satisfied:

1. Certainty
    o Understand the project purpose and outcome, strategy
    o Understand their own role and outcome
    o Have the ability to achieve outcome

2. Choice, variety, uncertainty
    o Allowed to make own decisions to achieve outcome if they want to
    o They are stretched if that's what they prefer
    o Are told what to do if they need to be
    o Are told why decisions are made that effect them

3. Significance
    o Feel important, in their role, themselves, as people
    o Feel listened to,
    o Feel their views are important

4. Connection Rapport
    o Feel part of team
    o Feel they can approach Project Manager and express views
    o Constructive feedback, team and personal performance, linked to outcome

5. Growth
   - o Are learning role
   - o Are developing, new understanding, skills, abilities
   - o Being mentored, coached

6. Contributing to success
   - o To their own success, career
   - o To team's success
   - o To the project success
   - o To their business' success

If all of the above are very positive and they
   - o Feel valuable, have the skills, experience, ability
   - o Feel valued by their peers, boos and business
     then they will be motivated to achieve their performance.

If all the project staff feel this way then the project will perform.

The Best Project Performance

Critical Chain Project Management

1 Produce traditional programme
   - o Logical diagram
   - o Detailed programme
   - o Clear task description
   - o Safety time within task
   - o Ensure logic is robust
   - o All tasks are logically connected
   - o Durations reflects the amount of effort, not elapsed time
   - o Resources are identified

2. Remove all safety time—reducing durations by 30-50%
3. Resolve any resource conflict
4. Identify the critical chain—through most overworked resource
5. Insert strategically place buffers
   - o Project buffer (PB), 1 number, to protect the completion date from slippage in critical chain
   - o Feeder buffers (FB), many, to protect the critical chain from slippages within the feeder lines
   - o Buffer sizes
     - • 1/3 of the critical chain (PB)
     - • 1/3 of the feeder lines (FB)

(buffer sizes can be adjusted to reflect risk)
6. Resources
  o Early warning for resources on critical chain
7. Buffer Management
  o Buffers split into traffic lights (PB & FB)
  o Monitor slippage into buffers
    • Frequently e.g. every 2 weeks
    • Green - watch
    • Orange - contingency plan
    • Red - implement contingency plan

Principles
  o No multi-tasking
  o Report duration to completion of tasks
  o Report early finishes
  o 100% of effort is required for all critical chain tasks
  o Need the required culture supported by project leader

The Best Project Solution

Every 3-6 months for a long project
  o Bring the team together, with the PM
  o Identify 3 key current problems for the project
  o Produce the conflict analysis for each of the 3 problems, in turn
    • Identify the undesired outcome UDO (box 1)
    • List why this is happening (box 2), full list, what is happening day to day, clarity, trends
    • Identify the desired outcome (DO) (box 3)
    • List why must we have the DO (box 4)
    • Identify the need for the UDO (box 5)
    • Identify the need for the DO (box 6)
    • Identify the joint objective (box 7)
    • Identify what is missing to resolve the list in 2 and overcome 1 (box 8)
  o Combine the 3 diagrams
  o Identify the core issue (all box 8s combined)

Implementation plan
  o Identify the target to overcome the core issue
  o Identify the plan of action, responsibilities and dates to achieve the target, logical diagram

Must have clarity of statements.

Must be done with Facilitator
Must be done with Project Manager and Project Team
Maximum 8 people

Chapter 9—Summary

What have you discovered about project management?

How can you apply this to your projects?

What ideas has it given you to improve your project management?

What are some actions you can take to start managing your projects to achieve the best possible outcome?

1.

2.

3.

4.

5.

Examples

10 Examples

All of these examples are based on actual projects and a number of organisations that I have been involved with. These examples have been slightly modified to ensure consistency of format, analysis, clarity to enable the reader to gain the best understanding.

10.1 Note sorting machine project

This example is a project that installs new machines to sorting money for a bank in an overseas country. This is based on a real project during 2006. The following is the project strategy that plans the project and plans how the project will be managed.

Introduction and context
The Central Bank, as one of its responsibilities, has to maintain currency of a certain quality in circulation. This requires that all the notes in circulation are required to be sorted enabling any unsatisfactory notes to be removed and replaced by new notes.

This process has become very inefficient because of the following factors:
- The note sorting machines are over 10 years old and unreliable.
- The currency has been considerably devalued requiring far greater number of notes to be in circulation and hence to be sorted. The sorting capacities of the machines are now inadequate top cope with this demand
- Currently the number of notes being sorted presently 55,000 notes per hour with an annual increase of 20%.
- The manufacturer no longer supports this type of machine and machine downtimes are long as all replacement parts have to be modified. When this occurs the staff have to work extended hours to clear the backlog of unprocessed notes.
- The machines work 24/7 to cope with the increasing demand

Purpose
To increase the note processing operation efficiency from 40% to 100% to achieve 110,000 notes per hour

Client's needs
The client is the Director of the bank. The banks corporate needs include:
- Double the efficiency of the note sorting process
- Minimise overtime, no week end working—less stressful staff
- More reliable machines and shorter downtimes, reduce costs—less stress on the maintenance technicians.
- Introduction of a 'state of the art' sorting process—In keeping with the bank's mission to be world class.

- o Feel confident in the project, the project team and project manager's abilities to implement this project.
- o Feel confident that the project will come in on time, within budget and at a very high quality.

The Director's personal needs include
- o Being kept informed with updated progress information, by the end of each week
- o Being immediately notified of incident that may prevent the project being achieved on time and achieving the increased efficiency

Problem to be overcome

This project is to overcome the note sorting process running at 40% of the volume of notes to be sorted, this is due to breakdowns, high maintenance, and also increase number of notes in circulation. Night working and weekend working is therefore required.

Outcome

The installation of high capacity bank note processing machines that are fully functional, all staff trained and the notes being processed.

Logical diagram

The logical diagram, Fig 10.1 defines what has to be in place that, collectively, will deliver the project outcome.

The logical diagram identifies:
- o sub-outcomes that will achieve the project outcome
- o logical must-have connections
- o the date for the achievement of the project outcome
- o the duration for each task, the of effort required to complete the task
- o who is responsibilities for carrying out each task, task owner
- o who is overall responsible, project manager

Detailed programme

Critical path programme (CP)

The logical diagram has been converted into a CP programme, Fig 10.2
- o each of the statements from that logical diagram have been restated in the programme
- o additional tasks have been identified that will achieve these statements
- o logic connections between the tasks have been robustly identified
- o the task durations have been included, 90% probability
- o the responsibilities for each task have been identified

Critical chain programme (CC)

The CCP programme has then been established, Fig 10.3, by
- o reducing the duration of each of the tasks by say 30%
- o the CC has been identified
- o the project buffer has been inserted to protect the completion date, logically connected with the required duration
- o feeder buffers have been inserted logically connected with the required duration

The CP programme has an overall duration of 53 days. The CC programme has been reduced to 45 days, giving considerable saving. This CC programme provides a shorter programme than the CP programme, by 8 days, thereby being able to win more contracts and achieve greater market share. However, to achieve this saving, then buffer management techniques were applied throughout the project to manage any slippage within the programme.

Benefits and Risks
The main benefits to the bank of implementing this project are:
- o cost savings of sorting the increasing numbers of notes
- o reduced maintenance costs
- o reduced overtime and week end working
- o improve staff morale
- o modern note sorting capability
- o the bank being seen as efficient

Some of the main risks to the non-achievement of the project outcome and benefits are:
- o insufficient capital to fund the project, errors in the calculation of the cost and benefits, causing the project to appear non-viable, or costs underestimated
- o incorrect machine specification resulting in sub-standard machines unable to process the notes at the required rate
- o the supplier not performing, units delayed, damaged, not properly installed delaying the project and budget overruns
- o staff not trained properly

The risks to the business if this project does not go ahead include:
- o costs are not reduced, the profits not achieved effecting the viability of the business
- o bank not been seen to be modernising and hence effecting reputation

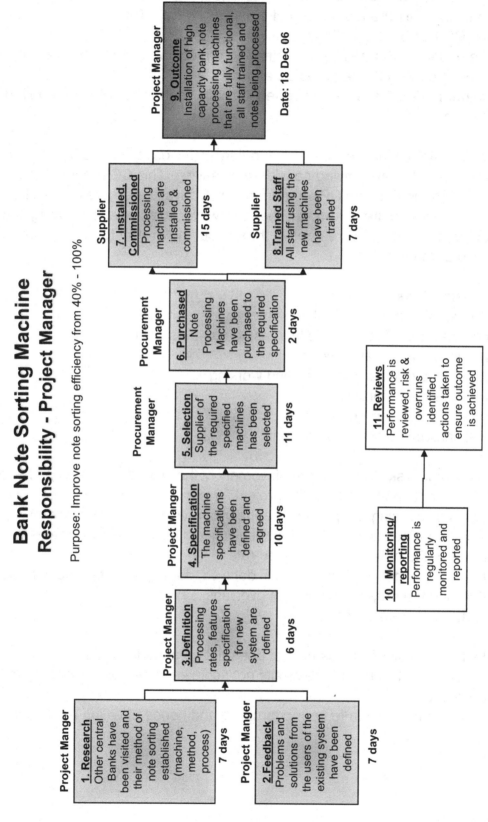

Fig 10.1 Logical diagram for Note Sorting Project

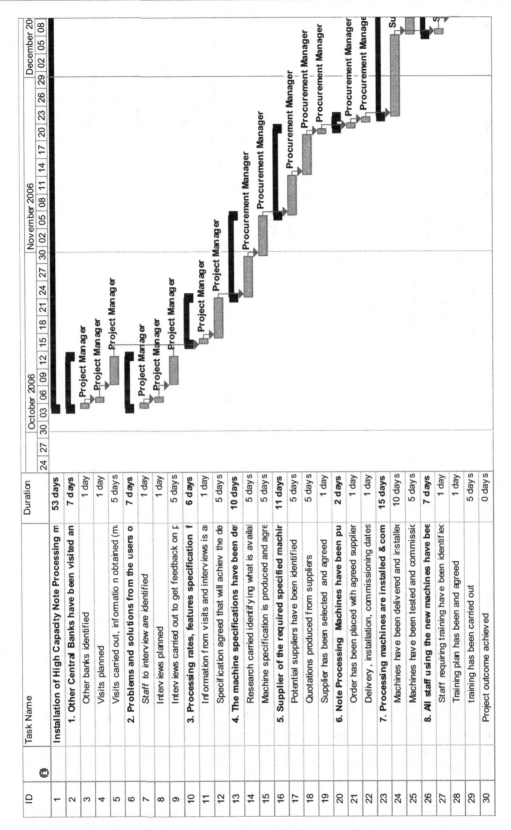

Fig 10.2 Critical path (CP) programme for Note Sorting project

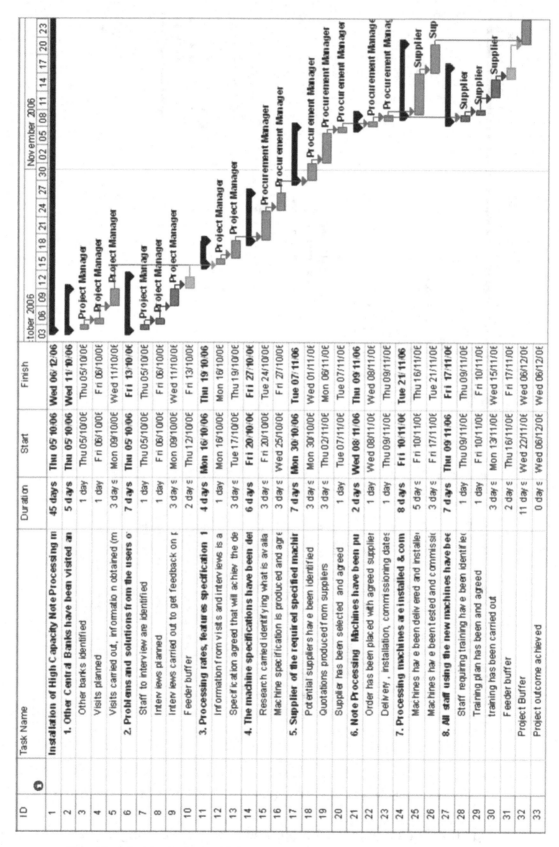

Fig 10.3 Critical chain (CC) programme for Note Sorting project

On the CC programme, fig 10.3, the project buffer is line 32. The feeder lines are 7,8,9 with a feeder buffer line 10, also a feeder line 28,29,30 with a feeder buffer line 31 which then links into the project buffer.

Roles and Responsibilities

The project organisation is shown on the organisation chart, fig 10.4, with clear reporting lines.

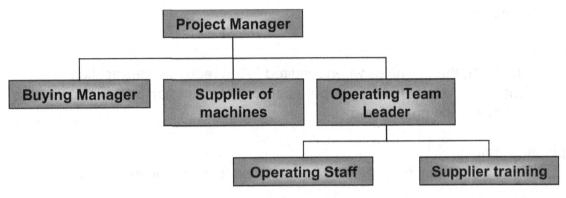

Fig 10.4 Organisation chart

The responsibilities include:-

Project Sponsor or Director
- o provides the funding for the project
- o regular reviews progress with the project manager
- o reports back to the main board the progress made

Project Manager
- o main role and responsibility is to achieve the project outcome "Installation of high capacity bank note processing machines that are fully functional, all staff trained and notes being processed" and thereby achieve the purpose of the project within the allocated budget
- o manage the project team, regularly communicate with them, so that they understand and achieve their own role within the project
- o manage the CC programme and ensure the tasks on the programme are achieved, managing any slippage into the buffers, so that the project is completed by the due date
- o plan and achieve own tasks identified on the logical diagram and CC programme
  - research
  - feedback
  - definition
  - specification

- o   analyse the risks of not achieving the project outcome on time and to budget
- o   carry out weekly reviews of the project performance with the team, measure and monitor performance and implement actions to ensure the project is delivered on time and to budget
- o   report progress and any slippage or concerns to the project sponsor

Procurement Manager
- o   Selection and purchasing of the specified machines within the budget and timescale

Supplier
- o   Supplying the machines when required to the required specification
- o   Training the staff to use and operate the machines to an agreed training plan that meets the programme

Operating staff
- o   To be competent and operate the machines to the required standard

Financial plan

The budget for the project is £118,000 and is made up of staff cost and the supply of the machines.

The budget profile is shown in Fig 10.5. This budget includes the costing of the feeder and project buffers, which amounts to £3,000. There is a financial risk buffer of £13,000 (staff cost buffer of £3,000 and machine cost buffer of £10,000). The intention is to not spend this amount, the project cost target is therefore £105,000.

Each week the project costs, staff and machine costs, will be calculated and presented on a cost profile. This cost will be compared to the budget profile and the cost target. A revised cost forecast will be produced.

Any overspend will be investigated and actions implemented, such as reducing the staff time to complete a task, to ensure the cost target is achieved. If the cost overruns cannot be recovered then any project overspend, with the revised cost forecast, will be reported to the project director.

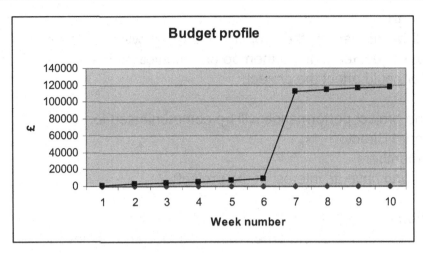

Fig 10.5 Budget profile

Monitoring and measures
The key measure that determines the success of the project is:
- o   whether the new machines achieves the 110,000 notes per hour

Other measures include:
- o   tasks completed against the critical chain programme, and duration to completion
- o   weekly measure of the amount of slippage into the feeder and project buffers as a percentage of the feeder lines and the critical chain
- o   weekly measure of the actual cost compared to target cost and budget profile, percentage cost buffers used up

Culture, values
The culture that is needed to ensure that this project is completed successfully is:
The project team are fully committed to work together, to deliver the programmed tasks in order to achieve a successful project outcome within the cost target. To achieve this we must have:
- o   complete honesty
- o   helping each other to achieve their tasks
- o   full commitment by all

Reviews and improvement plan
Reviews will be carried out weekly. A meeting will be held with the project team. As a team we will:
- o   review slippage into the feeder and project buffers
- o   review slippage into the cost buffers
- o   agree any actions necessary to bring the project aback on course to achieve the required project outcome and cost target.

Communication

This plan will be agreed by the project Director. It will then be communicated and agreed by the project team. It will then be communicated to those staff members who are affected or could affect the project.

Updates of the project performance will be communicated to
- o   the Board Director
- o   team members
- o   others who have an interest in the project

Project outcome

This project was completed on time, within budget and achieved the required note sorting target.

10.2 Training project

This project is to set up a new training regime on a large contract that has recently been won. The contract is for 5 years with approximately 500 staff. So this project is to set up and establish the contract training.

Introduction

This training strategy covers how the production staff training will be managed. It identifies the budget requirements for the financial year, the training requirements for the production staff, and how the training will be managed to ensure the outcome will be achieved.
This strategy will be updated at the beginning of each financial year.

Purpose

The purpose of the training is
   "Training complies with Health and Safety legislation and contract requirements"

It is illegal to put people to work without the statutory certification.

Outcome

The outcome of training is that:
   "All staff are formally inducted, trained and have the required competency to carry out work to the required standard"

Benefits and risks

The benefits of achieving this outcome and purpose include:-
- o   Improved company reputation
- o   Repeat orders and work from the Client

- o Satisfied staff who feel motivated and want to work for us
- o Comply with legislation and company standards

Also by implementing this strategy we will be developing a consistent approach to training across the contract.

Risks of not implementing this training strategy include:-

- o Risk of prosecution is not minimised
- o Risk of injury to our staff and 3rd parties is not minimised
- o Risk of the effects on company reputation not minimised
- o Risk of damage to 3rd party property, plant and the environment is not minimised

Logical Diagram

The logical diagram, Fig 10.6, describes what has to be in place to deliver the defined outcome.

The annual training plan, identified within the logical diagram, must be produced by the end of January for the coming financial year. This enables the co-ordination of the training course to be planned, cost effectively, to minimise risk.

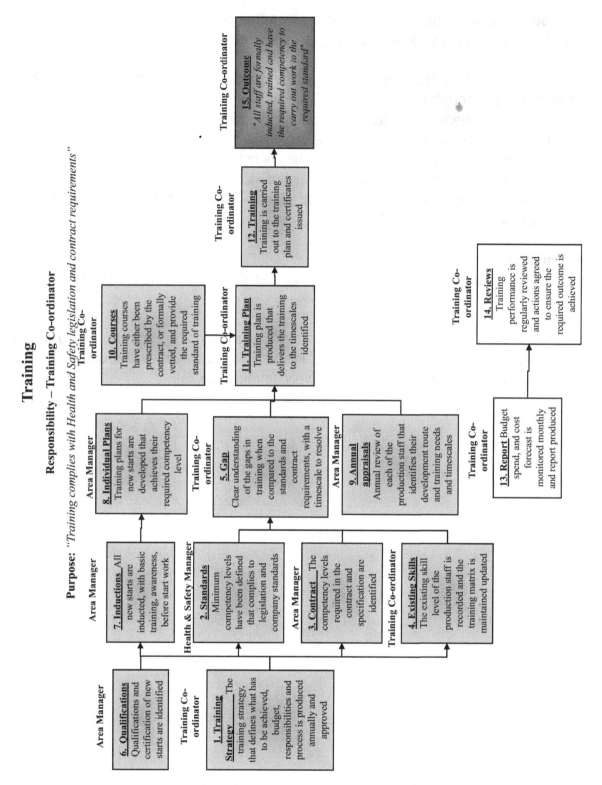

Fig 10.6 Training logical diagram

Detailed programme

The logical diagram has been converted into a critical path programme (CP), Fig 10.8.This shows 85days period for the project. The training plan is the key milestone, giving a key date of 27th April. there is a fairly high risk of overrunning this due date.

A critical chain programme (CC) has been produced that reduces the duration of each task, identifies the critical chain, inserts project and feeder buffers. This programme is presented in Fig 10.9. This shows a project duration of 63 days, a saving of 22 days on the programme when compared to the CP. This foreshortened programme will only be achieved if buffer management techniques are used.

Roles and responsibilities

The logical diagram identifies the role that key people need to have implemented in order to achieve the outcome.
These responsibilities include:
- o Training Co-ordinator
- o Training liaisons
- o Area Manager
- o Construction Team

Budget, Cost forecast and reporting

The annual budget has been agreed to be £360k for the contract duration.
This includes a rate for
- o each production staff of—£1400 per person
- o each support staff of—£600 per person

This budget will be reviewed at the start of each financial year.

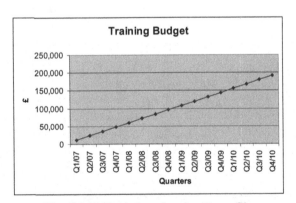

Fig 10.7 Training budget profile

The actual cost profile of the training will be reviewed at the end of each quarter and compared with the budget profile. A cost forecast will be produced predicting the actual cost of the training for the financial year. Any projected overspend of the budget will be reported and agreed

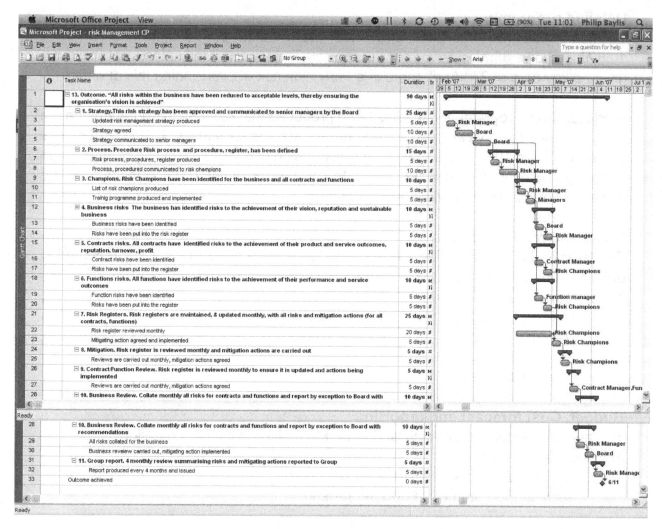

Fig 10.8 Training Project Critical Path programme

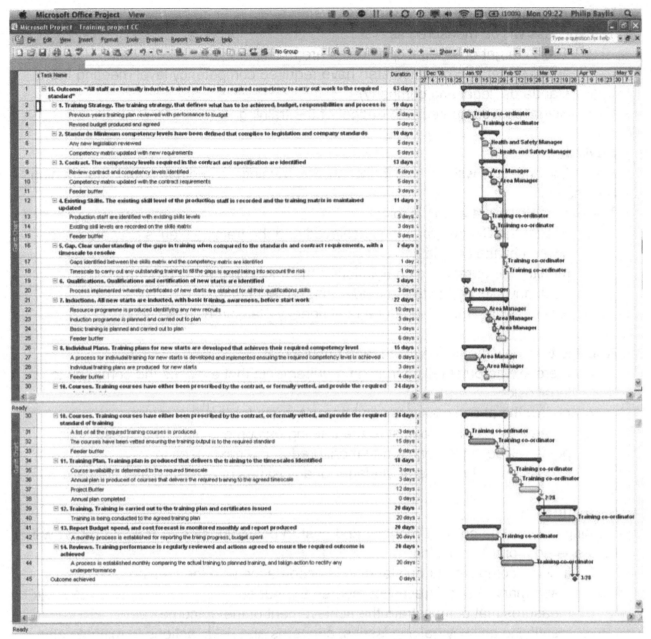

Fig 10.9 Training Project Critical Chain programme

The project buffer in, fig 10.9, is shown in line 37 and is approximately 1/3 of the critical chain. The feeder buffers are shown in lines 11, 15, 25, 29, 33 and they are 1/3 of their respective feeder lines.

Measures, monitoring and reporting

The success will be measured as:-

- o   100 % target of all legal certificates are maintained and kept in date
- o   100% target of production staff have required competency level meeting the standards (legal and company)
- o   Actual cost compared with budget of the training

Reviews

A monthly meeting will be held between the training co-ordinator and the training liaisons.

The purpose of this meeting is to:

- o   ensure the CC programme is achieved and the training plan is prepared and agreed by the due date
- o   monitor the duration to completion of the tasks on the CC programme
- o   track any slippage in to the feeder and project buffers
- o   green—wait; amber—produce contingency plans; red—take action

Also it is to review the training plan, and ensure that:

- o   there are no outstanding training requirements that exposes the company to legal risk
- o   review the above measures and agree targets for the next month
- o   agree actions plans to ensure the training outcome is achieved, these action plans will be implemented and monitored at the next meeting
- o   escalation to the General Manager of any issues of exposure and concern

Reporting

Training cost will be collated monthly and cost forecast updated. A training report will be prepared monthly including:

- o   training completed or outstanding in accordance with the training plan
- o   a summary of cost forecast compared to budget
- o   measures that demonstrate the achievement of the outcome
- o   identifying any key training issues, concerns and risks, actions to mitigate any risks

The report will be issued to the Director, Area Managers, training liaisons and Construction Manager.

Communications

This training strategy will be agreed with the Director and communicated to Area Managers, training liaisons and Construction Manager.

The annual training plan will be issued to Director, Area Managers, training liaisons and Construction Manager.

The monthly training report will be communicated to Director, Area Managers, training liaisons and Construction Manager.

10.3 Risk management project

This project involved setting up a risk management approach within the business. Whilst there were aspects of risk management being carried out throughout the business, it was inconsistent and sporadic. It was this inconsistency in the process and the management of the actual risks that was the major issue. The international group were unaware of the aggregate risks that their business was exposed to.

Introduction
This risk management strategy explains how risk is to be managed within the organisation in accordance with the Group's philosophy.

Purpose
The purpose of this initiative is

"to provide a consistent approach to the management and mitigating of risk across the business, reflecting the Group's approach to risk management"

Definition of risk
The risks that are considered in this strategy include:

Overall business risks to:
- o the achievement of the projected turnover for the next few years
- o achievement of the required profit
- o effects on reputation

Contractual risks include:
- o achieving the contractual requirements
- o ensuring the operations achieve the required performance
- o ensuring the health, safety, environmental, and quality legislation and standards are achieved
- o satisfying our commercial obligations
- o ensuring we achieve the required profitability
- o ensuring we achieve the required income
- o ensuring accuracy of cost forecasting and monitoring
- o ensuring performance delivery
- o minimising and effects on 3rd party

Central support office risks include:
- o winning work to achieve the required turnover
- o providing support enabling the supply chain to perform

o providing support for our people
o ensuring the financial analysis is accurate and timely
o ensuring the required transport is provided
o ensuring sufficient understanding, support and systems for health, safety, environment and quality

Outcome
The Outcome of this risk management strategy is:
"All risks within the business have been reduced to acceptable levels, thereby ensuring the organisation's vision is achieved"

Benefits and risks
The benefits of implementing this strategy include:
o Consistent approach to risk management
o Compliant to group requirements
o Risks are reduced to acceptable levels

This will have a knock on benefit to the business of
o Minimising costs, waste
o Reducing claims
o Assisting in achieving a successful business and turnover and profit
o The business becomes more marketable and hence increase market share
o Demonstrating to the Group that we are leading the approach to risk management, and hence recognition from the Group

Logical diagram
The logical diagram that defines what has to be in place to achieve the project outcome is identified in Fig 10.10

Risks to achieving this logical diagram include
o The Board not approving the risk strategy
o The Board not communicating the strategy to the contract and functional managers
o The Board not demonstrating full commitment and insisting on risk reports and mitigating action
o The contract and functional mangers not supporting this initiative
o Structured and frequent reviews not being conducted

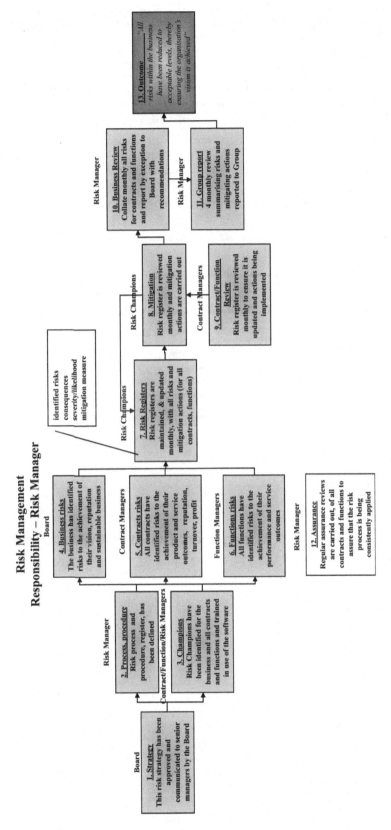

Fig 10.10 Risk management logical diagram

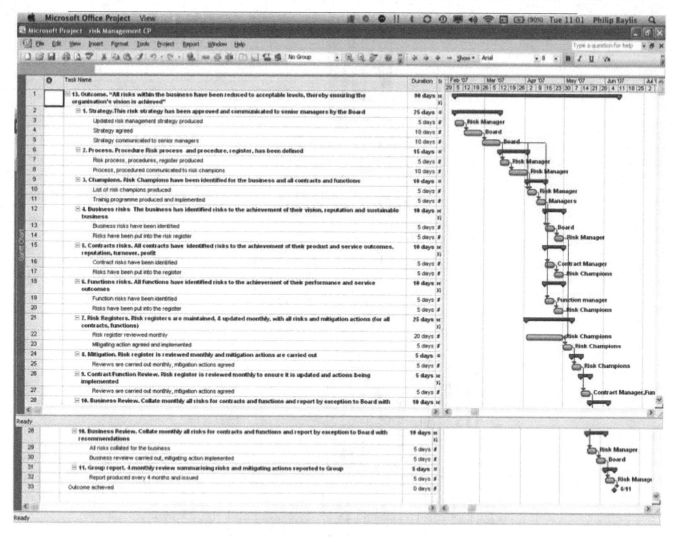

Fig 10.11 Risk Management Critical Path programme

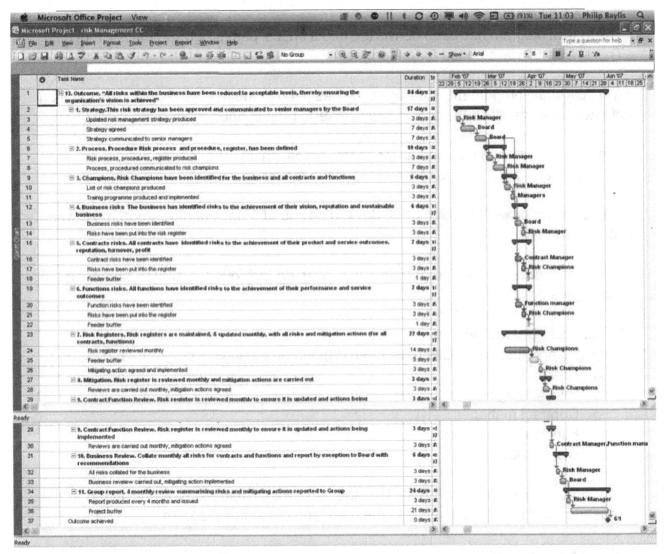

Fig 10.12 Risk Management Critical Chain programme

Detailed programme

The logical diagram has been converted into a critical path programme (CP), Fig 10.11. This shows 90 days period for the project.

A critical chain programme (CC), fig 10.12, has been produced that reduces the duration of each task, identifies the critical chain, inserts project and feeder buffers.

The project buffer line 36 and is 1/3 of the critical chain. The feeder buffers are lines 18, 22, 25 and each are 1/3 of their respective feeder lines.

This shows a project duration of 84 days, a saving of 6 days on the programme when compared to the CP.

This foreshortened CC programme will only be achieved if buffer management techniques are used.

Roles and responsibilities

The roles and responsibilities have been defined on the logical diagram, and include:
  o Board
  o Risk Manager
  o Contract manager
  o Functional manager
  o Risk Champions

The job descriptions for the Risk Manager and Risk Champions are included in the appendix, and are linked directly to the roles and outcomes diagram.

Risk Manager Role:

Role Outcome (Refer to logical diagram Fig 10.10):
All risks within the business have been reduced to acceptable levels, thereby ensuring the business vision is achieved.

Ensure the Group philosophy is complied to.

Actions
  o Process - Define the Risk process and procedure, define the risk register system structure
  o Training - Train champions to use the software
  o Assurance - Carry out reviews 4 monthly, of all contracts and functions to assure that the risks are being identified and mitigated
  o Business Review - Collate monthly all risks for contracts and functions and report by exception to Board with recommendations

- o Group—4 monthly review summarising risks and mitigating actions reported to Group
- o Annual Opportunities and Risk Management Review—Annual review of opportunities and risks summarising all risks and laying out annual targets

Risk Champions Role:

Role Outcome

Risk register for the contract/function is maintained and updated monthly, with all risks and mitigation actions.

Actions
- o identify risks
- o identify consequences
- o identify severity/likelihood
- o identify mitigation measure
- o identify who is responsible
- o ensure mitigation action is carried out

Prepare and maintain the risk register updated, and also 4 monthly opportunity and risk reviews, in accordance with the process and procedures and Group philosophy.

Measures, monitoring and reporting

The measure of success of this risk project includes:
- o The actions on the logical diagram will be monitored each month for each contract and function demonstrating the success of implementation of this project
- o Number of red risks
- o Number of mitigating actions to reduce the risks to an acceptable level

Monthly report will be completed to the standard format for
- o Each contract
- o Each function

Report issued to Group every quarter

10.4 Process Software Implementation Project

1. The way it was

The business was a £500m turnover, with a head office and 10 external project offices.

The head office included all of the normal functions including Health and Safety, Human Resources, Finance.

The external project offices were situated across the country. The projects were multi-million pounds, lasting 2-5 years, occasionally up to 10 years.

The software in this case was a process mapping software. The decision to implement was by the CEO, top down. The objective was to "*Implement the Software*" across the complete business, including in the head office and on all project offices. The plan was for all processes to be mapped and all aspects of the business and projects to be carried out in a consistent manner.

The rollout approach was to set up the software and carry out training on how to use the software across all of the project offices and head office simultaneously, a bow wave.

There were controls from centre of the style and format protocols, and the instruction was to map processes bottom up in detail. So all of the projects mapped their processes in detail, creating 100s of process maps on each project, many layers. Using a standard style which limited the number of boxes per view/page/maps, colouring not allowed, inputs & outputs. This was regularly reported upwards to the CEO.

Much time and money has been spent on its implementation, £500k of money for external services such as licenses and training support, another £500k taken up in staff time such as attending training, carrying out mapping workshops.

After 2 years of implementation everyone in all project offices, and in the head office, has the software on their computers and have been trained on its use. So in this sense the objective has been achieved.

However, has there been a benefit to the implementation of this software, has the business improved its performance? No, not to date. Will there be? Probably not.

What has been the return of investment? None that can be demonstrated to date.

What is the feeling or views of this software? There is resistance, frustration, the people involved are continually question the value of the software.
The damage has been done, it will be a lot harder to overcome this resistance and to achieve any benefit at all. The way it was project managed created the resistance within people.

Effectively there was no direction. Every one was complying with the instructions and the objective, but they were pointing in different directions.

The project lived in isolation to the business.

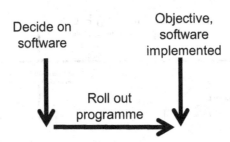

Fig 10.13 The software roll out programme is not connected
to business performance

2. The way it should have been

When discussing these issues and understanding why the software had to be implemented it transpired that the **purpose** was to:

"To protect the Directors of the business from corporate manslaughter by having consistent statutory related processes across the business and contract offices"

or to be more succinct *"To be legally compliant"*

The **outcome** would have been
"All statutory related processes, H&S, HR, Finance, have been defined, mapped, agreed and being applied across the complete business, including all contract offices"

To do this then the focus of attention need only have been on the head office where the Health and Safety, HR, and Finance departments were based. If their processes were defined and agreed, and then all project offices would be instructed to comply with the any training necessary. This would only have taken 3-4 months, at a fraction of the time and cost, whilst achieving the outcome and purpose.

This is how the *Power of Purpose* will create the focus, it provides direction, that will minimise waste and achieves performance.

At the start of the initiative then the team implementing this initiative should have been brought together to define the project, including the purpose and outcome.

The project would be set up as follows:

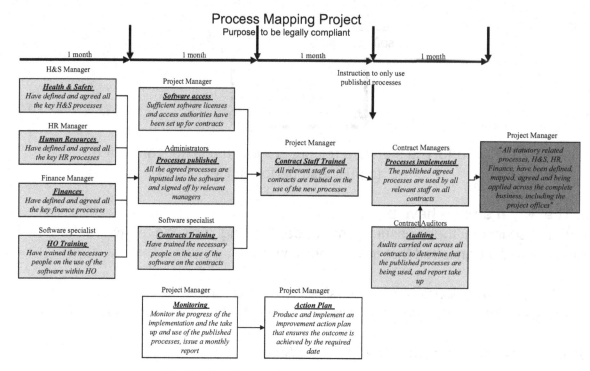

Fig 10.14 The software logical diagram

Throughout this initiative the team must continually ask

- Are our decisions aligned to our purpose?
- Are what we are doing aligned to our purpose?
- Are the maps that we are producing aligned to our purpose?
- Are those people that we are involved with aligned, understand our purpose?
- Are we monitoring and reporting against the outcome

The culture of the implementation team must also be aligned to the purpose.
The values statement would be

"We as a team are committed to working together, are enthusiastic and are focused to deliver this project and achieve the outcome and purpose within the timescale"

If the cultural values align to the purpose then the project is likely to be implemented in the most effective way.

So the *purpose* provides the direction for people involved to align themselves to.

Here the project is a business performance related project, and the software is linked to the outcome.

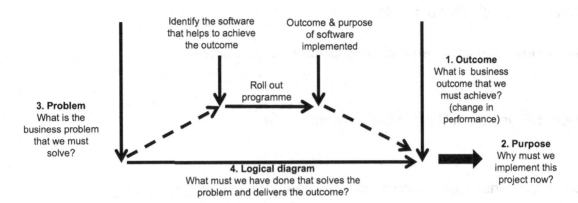

Fig 10.15 The roll out programme connecting the software to improved business performance

Chapter 10—Project examples

What have you discovered about project management?

How can you apply this to your projects?

What ideas has it given you to improve your project management?

What are some actions you can take to start managing your projects to achieve the best possible outcome?

1.

2.

3.

4.

5.

11   Testimonials

"This book provides a stimulating alternative approach to delivering successful projects. A few key areas are discussed, but they build towards an overall picture of the essential management activity to deliver infrastructure projects. Philip draws on theory, and his own accumulated experience, to provide a valuable guide for students and practitioners of project management."

Pete Harpum, Managing Director, Harpum Consulting

"I have worked with Phil for some time, he has been a significant help. Through strategic thinking he has helped me to clearly define my business vision and the journey that has to be in place to deliver that vision. The concepts and ideas in this book have provided a valuable tool for my onward journey"

Darren Nelson, Owner, Carnell Contractors Ltd

"The overall message is correct, i.e. the best project outcomes must be a combination of using PM methodology best practice and other factors such as organisational alignment and appropriate leadership/governance support etc.

Specifically how I think your book helps a PM is by simplifying and de-mystifying what the critical factors for success are for the project. Your book could be used as a reference guide on how to frame a successful project very quickly, which is a fundamental part of all projectised delivery (i.e. getting things going quickly). The PM should also benefit from being able to identify who to engage on the project to give himself a better chance of succeeding (basic stakeholder management really, but often not performed as a matter of course).

Viewing your book from the business perspective, I see the benefit to the business being one of reducing the overall risk profile of running multiple projects (linked or not). The business should be able to build capability and maturity more effectively and efficiently using the concepts and information presented in your book.

I expect the overall impact of the above to be one of improved delivery and financial performance (i.e. fewer projects dealing with unplanned variances). Clearly, this will benefit the organisation from several fronts: financial, organisational capability and people performance to name a few but there will be other benefits too.

Using your book must help the organisation to become not only a better performing organisation but also perceived in the market place as a better performing organisation which is likely to enhance credibility and potentially sales.

Without doubt, your book needs to be read and understood by any organisation that is projectised in its form (i.e. not operationalised). This means those in the Project Management community and all those stakeholders of projects MUST read your book"

Manou Amirpashaie, Project Manager, Fujitsu

"The examples are excellent and a good road map for any up and coming manager looking for leadership and guidance, but one has to remember that large Corporates have their own tried & tested systems and do not like employees straying from the Company line, so that it is vital that his book gets accepted at the highest of levels!

I would expect huge improvements in implementation, continuity and performance as the book can be used as an excellent template for an organisation to work from ensuring peak performance and a complete approach to potentially expensive problems.

I recommend this book to all Project Managers, Development Managers/Directors, MD's & CEO's of any organisation that wants to progress and grow"

Martin Parkes, Managing Director, Parkes and Son

"An excellent book for anyone wanting to achieve the best possible results, benefits and value from any project that ensures people, processes and performance are effective and optimised

I would make this book a basic requirement for every project leader and manager to study and ensure they fully understand and practice these principles.

I fully support and recommend the use of the modelling and profiling tools at the earliest stages of any project making comparisons to the ideal role models.

What this book provides is the opportunity for any construction and project management company to possess the framework for quality of approach to ensure the best possible outcome.

I will certainly recommend this book to all my clients"

Dan Patey, Senior Partner DND Associates

12   References

Association for Project Management (1999) The APM Body of Knowledge. APM, UK.

Bandler, R. and Grindler, J. Neuro Linguistic Programming

Baylis, P. (1998) Project Constraints. The application of "Critical Chain" to Project Management in construction at a 4 day Jonah International Symposium,—May 1998, London

Baylis, P. (2001) Achieving Project Performance. Managing the effects of uncertainty on I) due date performance, ii) financial performance. Personal material on critical chain course

BS 6079-1:2002 Project management—Part 1: Guide to project management.

Burke, Rory (2003) Project Management, Planning and Control Techniques Fourth Edition, Wiley, 0-470-85124-4

Covey, S. R., (1999) Principle Centred Leadership Simon & Schuster UK Ltd 1992 reissued 1999.

Gibbs, Eddie. (2008) Leadership Next, Changing Leaders in a Changing Culture, Church. Inter-Varsity Press

Goldratt E.M. (1990). Theory of Constraints. North River Press, New York

Goldratt E.M., Cox, J (1984) The Goal. (1993) Second edition. Gower. 0-566-07418

Goldratt E.M. (1994) It's Not Luck. Gower. 0-566-07637-3

Goldratt E.M. (1997) Critical Chain. The North River Press. Great Barrington, MA 0-88427-153-6

Goldratt E.M. (2000) Necessary but not Sufficient. The North River Press, Great Barrington, MA

http://www.goldratt.com/balfour.htm

Harpum, Pete Personal communication 2002

Hutchin, Dr. Ted, (2001) Enterprise-focused management, changing the face of project management. Thomas Telford 0-7277-2979-9

Hutchin, Dr T, (2002) Constraint Management in Manufacturing. Optimising the global supply chain. Taylor & Francis

Kerzner, Harold (2003) Project Management Workbook to Accompany Project Management, A Systems Approach to Planning, Scheduling, and Controlling Eighth Edition, Wiley. 0-471-22579-7

Leach, L. P. (2000) Critical Chain Project Management. Artech House 1 58053 074 5

Mantel, Samuel J. JR, Meredith, Jack R., Shafer, Scott M., and Sutton, Margaret M., (2001) Core Concepts of Project Management, Wiley 0-471-46606-9

Meredith, Jack R., and Mantel, Samuel J. JR, (2003) Project Management A managerial Approach Fifth Edition, Wiley 0471429074

Morris, P. W. G. Research at Oxford into the preconditions of success and failure in major projects. Proc. Project Management Institute Seminar/Symp. On Measuring Success, Montreal, 1986, Project Management Institute, Drexel Hill, PA, 1986.

Morris, P. (1994) The Management of Projects. Thomas Telford.

Morris, P. W. G. and Hough, G.H. The Anatomy of Major Projects. A Study of the Reality of Project Management. (1987) Wiley. 0-471-91551-3

Morris, Peter W. G. and Pinto, Jeffrey K. The Wiley Guide to Managing Projects (2004), John Wiley and Sons.

Newbold, RC. (1998) Project Management in the Fast Lane. Applying the Theory of Constraints. The St. Lucie Press/APICS on Constraints Management. 1-57444-195-7

Northouse, Petyer G. (2013) Leadership, Theory and Practice. 6th edition. SAGE

Patey, Dan. (2002) An Executive Development Programme: The Power of Executive Development Manual. How to create the future Executives who create real benefit and value. 18 Training Modules. www.DNDA.com

Patey, Dan (June 2003) Discover How to Sow the Seeds of Success. Putting The "U" In Success. Available electronically from www.DNDA.com

Pinto, J. and Kharbanda, O. P. (1995) Successful Project Managers: Leading your Team to Success. Van Nostrand Reinhold, New York. P225-243

Pinto, J. K. and Slevin, D. P., (1988) Critical success factors across the project life cycle, Project Management journal X1X (3), 67-7

Project Management Institute (PMI) (2013) A Guide to the Project Management Body of Knowledge (PMBOK Guide), 5th Edition www.pmi.org

Robbins, A. Unlimited power

Robbins, A. (2001) Awaken the Giant within. Pocket Books. 0-7434-0938-8

Robbins, A. Unleash the Power Within. Psychology of Peak Performance. Personal coaching to transform your life. Set of 6 CDs from Nightingale Conant. www.nightingale.com

Robbins, A. Unleash your Personal Power. Personal Power 2. The driving Force. Set of 25 CDs from Nightingale Conant. www.nightingale.com

Scheinkopf, L.J. Thinking for a Change. The St. Lucie Press/APICS on Constraints Management.1-57444-101-9

Smith, D. (2000) The Measurement Nightmare. How the Theory of Constraints Can Resolve Conflicting Strategies, Policies, and Measures. The St. Lucie Press/APICS on Constraints Management.1-57444-246-5